# The Limits of Language

*I gotta use words when I talk to you.*

—T. S. Eliot

# The Limits of Language

*Edited, with an Introduction*

*by*

WALKER GIBSON

*American Century Series*

HILL AND WANG · NEW YORK

Manufactured in the United States of America
by The Colonial Press Inc., Clinton, Massachusetts

# Acknowledgments

"Reflex Action and Theism" from *The Will to Believe and Other Essays* by William James, copyright 1897 by Longmans, Green & Company.

"The Organization of Thought" from *The Aims of Education* by Alfred North Whitehead, copyright 1929 by The Macmillan Company, renewed 1957 by Evelyn Whitehead. Used by permission of The Macmillan Company.

"The Changing Scientific Scene" from *Modern Science and Modern Man* by James B. Conant, copyright 1953 by Columbia University Press. Reprinted by permission of the publishers.

"A Note on Methods of Analysis" from *Science and Criticism* by Herbert J. Muller, copyright 1943 by Yale University Press. Reprinted by permission of the publishers.

"The Way Things Are" from *The Way Things Are* by P. W. Bridgman, published by Harvard University Press, Cambridge, Mass., copyright 1959 by The President and Fellows of Harvard College. Reprinted by permission of the publishers.

"A Definition of Style" from *The Open Mind* by J. Robert Oppenheimer, copyright 1955 by Simon and Schuster, Inc. Reprinted by permission of the publishers.

"Existentialism" from *Existentialism* by Jean-Paul Sartre, translated by Bernard Frechtman, copyright 1948 by the Philosophical Library. Reprinted by permission of the publishers.

"The Testimony of Modern Art" from *Irrational Man* by William Barrett, copyright © 1958 by William Barrett. Reprinted by permission of Doubleday & Co., Inc.

"Parts of Speech and Punctuation" from *Lectures in America* by Gertrude Stein, copyright 1935 by The Modern Library, Inc. Reprinted by permission of Random House, Inc.

"The Waves" from *The Waves* by Virginia Woolf, copyright 1931 by Harcourt, Brace & World, Inc., renewed 1959 by Leonard Woolf. Reprinted by permission of the publishers.

"The Imperfect Paradise" ("The Idea of Order at Key West" copyright 1935, 1936, 1954 by Wallace Stevens; "The Poems of Our Climate" copyright 1942, 1954 by Wallace Stevens; "Add This to Rhetoric" copyright 1942, 1954 by Wallace Stevens) from *The Collected Poems of Wallace Stevens*. Reprinted by permission of Alfred A. Knopf, Inc.

# Contents

# Introduction

THIS is a book about some difficulties and peculiarities of using language in our time. Whether these difficulties are in fact new, or have simply become aggravated in our century, the fact is that many people today are worried about words. The claim of this book on the reader's attention is that it collects within two covers several short pieces of writing concerned with some problems of modern expression. It is a book for the general reader who is concerned about his own expression, and would understand and apply to his own use some of the thinking that has been going on for some time now about the way words are employed to describe experience.

We begin with William James, lecturing as a young scientist to a group of Unitarian ministers in 1881. James reminds us that our raw experience, as it comes to us, is "an utter chaos." "While I talk and the flies buzz, a sea gull catches a fish at the mouth of the Amazon, a tree falls in the Adirondack wilderness, a man sneezes in Germany . . ." This meaningless mass of contemporary happenings is "the real order of the world" —and what we have to do to make sense of things is to *break* that order, by an act of will, and so create for our own human purposes new orders that are drastically different from the chaos of our immediate world. Thirty-five years later, Whitehead makes the same point: "I insist on the radically untidy, ill-adjusted character of the fields of actual experience from which science starts. To grasp this fundamental truth is the first step in wisdom." The fact is concealed, he says, by language, "which foists on us exact concepts as though they represented the immediate deliverance of experience." However indispensable language is, therefore, Whitehead sees it first as obscuring, hiding, isolating us from the way we actually do take in what we know.

Some even wider applications of this "fundamental truth" are suggested in following selections, where several modern scientists testify to the difficulties of expression inherent in their work. Just as the nature of "actual experience" cannot be rendered very accurately in words, so the nature of nature herself resists expression. Problems of definition arise that seem weird to the layman, such as the well-known paradox about light, which has to be considered as either particles or waves, depending on the operations of one's particular experiment. In a sentence quoted by James B. Conant in our third passage, "We can no longer say, The World is like this, or the World is like that." Herbert J. Muller in our fourth passage shows how the difficulties encountered by some modern scientists carry implications for us all, and that to speak in absolutes, sheep-or-goats, is an intellectual error that we have to avoid as the scientists have had to avoid it. The late P. W. Bridgman, Nobel prize-winning physicist, asserts a corollary implication for the user of words. Confronting these complexities, Bridgman concludes that one must be very aware of one's own limited point of view, the "first-person-singular" aspect of everything we say. This is the way it seems to me here at this moment. An application of such self-consciousness to the problem of style is summed up in a single paragraph (sixth passage) by J. Robert Oppenheimer. Style becomes "the deference that action pays to uncertainty."

The consequences of these difficulties extend far beyond the activities of scientists, as we have said, and the second part of this book presents a variety of such consequences. Philosophers, writers, painters, and ordinary citizens have been living for a long time now with the knowledge that a good deal of life is inexpressible. In the absence, for many people nowadays, of any absolute sanction to give us the Word, it becomes necessary to create our own (lower case) *words*, to make our own definitions, as best we can. The resulting responsibility for each individual person can be enormous; in Jean-Paul Sartre's famous phrase, we are "condemned to freedom." Our seventh passage offers Sartre describing individual responsibility from his "existentialist" point of view. A discussion of how modern painters have dealt with analogous difficulties in their art occupies the eighth passage, while the ninth is addressed to some questions about grammar and usage provoked by the kind of world we think we live in. Novelists and poets, of course, have been responding to "the limits of language" for centuries, but they have done so recently with characteristic self-consciousness. In their different ways, a selection from Virginia Woolf's *The Waves* and three poems by Wallace Stevens demonstrate a twentieth-century concern with problems of language and reality.

Obviously all these passages were selected to present a particular set of qualities and difficulties in modern expression, and no doubt other passages might have been selected to present other qualities and difficulties. Furthermore no introductory and nontechnical book of this length can hope to be adequate for the linguistic specialist or the historian of ideas. Naturally the reader is free to disagree with the attitudes toward language and life represented here. He may argue that these attitudes are pessimistic, or agnostic, or hard to live with—as indeed they generally are. A kind of "anti-rational" prejudice informs this book, an attitude that expresses, someone has said, a tragic view of language. Perhaps so. The reader is welcome to whatever more satisfactory version of things he can discover. But at least so far as these passages testify, the familiar pressures of our particular scientific age do not very clearly offer anything easier, more solid or comfortable. There can be genuine comfort in another direction: in the recognition of man's own freedom and power, limited and lonely though they may be. For what it may be worth—and I think it is worth a great deal—man is left master of whatever it is he can make himself master of.

We return finally to style. The consequences of this freedom and this limitation for the everyday user of words—the teacher, the student, the citizen—are real but unexplored. They may come down in the end to some devices of rhetoric —irony, for instance, through which one suggests to one's listener the restricted application and reliability of what one is saying. In a note at the end of this book, I try to say something about these stylistic consequences, but I do so, I hope, conscious of my own ironical situation. There is an obvious hazard in any man's effort to tell any other man, in language, about the limits of language. The line from Eliot that appears as epigraph to this book sardonically footnotes everything we say: "I gotta use words when I talk to you."

# NATURE OF THE PROBLEM:
## Testimony from Scientists

# WILLIAM JAMES

## 1: Reflex Action and Theism

*A prevailing interest of this book is the impact of science, or of a certain sort of scientist, on other areas of life, on beliefs and attitudes and most of all words, in the arts and in everyday existence. In the following excerpt from a lecture delivered in 1881 to a group of Unitarian ministers, William James identifies himself as a "teacher of physiology," and he seeks, with the modesty and good humor the reader will witness, to connect some current work in biology with the concerns of his liberally religious audience. As his opening remarks show, new developments in science were already, in 1881, almost too fashionable a subject of popular enthusiasm.*

*The reader who knows his present-day biology will probably find James's account of reflex action primitive, but if so, he is to remember that we are concerned here with defining an attitude toward language, and not with "the latest breeze from the physiological horizon." Of first importance for our purposes is James's assertion of the chaotic given order of experience, and the role of man's subjective will in "breaking" and so controlling that chaos. The entire lecture, of course, has its other interests, and the reader is invited to consult it all as printed in* The Will to Believe and Other Essays in Popular Philosophy.

*Born in 1842, James was not yet forty, a scientist at Harvard, when this lecture was delivered. The philosophical interests*

3

*that were later to make him famous are already discernible here, of course, even though his great works in philosophy* (Varieties of Religious Experience, Pragmatism) *did not appear until the early years of this century.*

Members of the Ministers' Institute:

Let me confess to the diffidence with which I find myself standing here today. When the invitation of your committee reached me last fall, the simple truth is that I accepted it as most men accept a challenge—not because they wish to fight, but because they are ashamed to say no. Pretending in my small sphere to be a teacher, I felt it would be cowardly to shrink from the keenest ordeal to which a teacher can be exposed—the ordeal of teaching other teachers. Fortunately, the trial will last but one short hour; and I have the consolation of remembering Goethe's verses:

> *Vor den Wissenden sich stellen,*
> *Sicher ist 's in allen Fällen,*

for if experts are the hardest people to satisfy, they have at any rate the liveliest sense of the difficulties of one's task, and they know quickest when one hits the mark.

Since it was as a teacher of physiology that I was most unworthily officiating when your committee's invitation reached me, I must suppose it to be for the sake of bringing a puff of the latest winds of doctrine which blow over that somewhat restless sea that my presence is desired. Among all the healthy symptoms that characterize this age, I know no sounder one than the eagerness which theologians show to assimilate results of science, and to hearken to the conclusions of men of science about universal matters. One runs a better chance of being listened to today if one can quote Darwin and Helmholtz than if one can only quote Schleiermacher or Coleridge. I almost feel myself this moment that were I to produce a frog and put him through his physiological performances in a masterly manner before your eyes, I should gain more reverential ears for what I have to say during the remainder of the hour. I will not ask whether there be not something of mere fashion in this prestige which the words of the physiologists enjoy just now. If it be a fashion, it is certainly a beneficial one upon the whole; and to challenge it would come with a poor grace from one who at the moment he speaks is so conspicuously profiting by its favors.

I will therefore only say this: that the *latest* breeze from the physiological horizon need not necessarily be the most important one. Of the immense amount of work which the laboratories of Europe and America, and one may add of Asia and Australia, are producing every year, much is destined to speedy refutation; and of more it may be said that its interest is purely technical, and not in any degree philosophical or universal.

This being the case, I know you will justify me if I fall back on a doctrine which is fundamental and well established rather than novel, and ask you whether by taking counsel together we may not trace some new consequences from it which shall interest us all alike as men. I refer to the doctrine of reflex action, especially as extended to the brain. This is, of course, so familiar to you that I hardly need define it. In a general way, all educated people know what reflex action means.

It means that the acts we perform are always the result of outward discharges from the nervous centers, and that these outward discharges are themselves the result of impressions from the external world, carried in along one or another of our sensory nerves. Applied at first to only a portion of our acts, this conception has ended by being generalized more and more, so that now most physiologists tell us that every action whatever, even the most deliberately weighed and calculated, does, so far as its organic conditions go, follow the reflex type. There is not one which cannot be remotely, if not immediately, traced to an origin in some incoming impression of sense. There is no impression of sense which, unless inhibited by some other stronger one, does not immediately or remotely express itself in action of some kind. There is no one of those complicated performances in the convolutions of the brain to which our trains of thought correspond, which is not a mere middle term interposed between an incoming sensation that arouses it and an outgoing discharge of some sort, inhibitory if not exciting, to which itself gives rise. The structural unit of the nervous system is in fact a triad, neither of whose elements has any independent existence. The sensory impression exists only for the sake of awaking the central process of reflection, and the central process of reflection exists only for the sake of calling forth the final act. All action is thus *re*-action upon the outer world; and the middle stage of consideration or contemplation or thinking is only a place of transit, the bottom of a loop, both of whose ends have their point of application in the outer world. If it should ever have no roots in the outer world, if it should ever happen that it led to no active measures, it would fail of its essential function, and would have to be considered either pathological or abortive. The current of life which runs in at our eyes or ears is meant to run out at our hands, feet, or lips. The only use of the thoughts it occasions while inside is to determine its direction to whichever of these organs shall, on the whole, under the circumstances actually present, act in the way most propitious to our welfare.

The willing department of our nature, in short, dominates both the conceiving department and the feeling department; or, in plainer English, perception and thinking are only there for behavior's sake.

I am sure I am not wrong in stating this result as one of the fundamental conclusions to which the entire drift of modern physiological investigation sweeps us. If asked what great contribution physiology has made to psychology of late years, I am sure every competent authority will reply that her influence has in no way been so weighty as in the copious illustration, verification, and consolidation of this broad, general point of view.

I invite you, then, to consider what may be the possible speculative consequences involved in this great achievement of our generation. Already, it dominates all the new work done in psychology; but what I wish to ask is whether its influence may not extend far beyond the limits of psychology, even into those of theology itself. The relations of the doctrine of reflex action with no less a matter than the doctrine of theism is, in fact, the topic to which I now invite your attention. . . .

But, first of all, let me ask you to linger a moment longer over what I have called the reflex theory of mind, so as to be sure that we understand it absolutely before going on to consider those of its consequences of which I am more particularly to speak. I am not quite sure that its full scope is grasped even by those who have most zealously promulgated it. I am not sure, for example, that all physiologists see that it commits them to regarding the mind as an essentially teleological mechanism. I mean by this that the conceiving or theorizing faculty—the mind's middle department—functions *exclusively for the sake of ends* that do not exist at all in the world of impressions we receive by way of our senses, but are set by our emotional and practical subjectivity altogether. It is a transformer of the world of our impressions into a totally different world—the world of our conception; and the transformation is effected in the interests of our volitional nature, and for no other purpose whatsoever. Destroy the volitional nature, the definite subjective purposes, preferences, fondnesses for certain effects, forms, orders, and not the slightest motive would remain for the brute order of our experience to be remodeled at all. But, as we have the elaborate volitional constitution we do have, the remodeling must be effected; there is no escape. The world's contents are *given* to each of us in an order so foreign to our subjective interests that we can hardly by an effort of the imagination picture to ourselves what it is like. We have to break that order altogether— and by picking out from it the items which concern us, and connecting them with others far away, which we say "belong" with them, we are able to make out definite threads of sequence and tendency; to foresee particular liabilities and get ready for them; and to enjoy simplicity and harmony in place of what was chaos. Is not the sum of your actual experience taken at this moment and impartially added together an utter chaos? The strains of my voice, the lights and shades inside the room and out, the murmur of the wind, the ticking of the clock, the various organic feelings you may happen individually to possess, do these make a whole at all? Is it not the only condition of your mental sanity in the midst of them that most of them should become nonexistent for you, and that a few others—the sounds, I hope, which I am uttering—should evoke from places in your memory that have nothing to do with this scene associates fitted to combine with them in what we call a rational train of thought—rational, because it leads to a conclusion which we have some organ to appreciate? We have no organ or faculty to appreciate the simply given order. The real world as it is given objectively at this moment is the sum total of all its being and events now. But can we think of such a sum? Can we realize for an instant what a cross-section of all existence at a definite point of time would be? While I talk and the flies buzz, a sea gull catches a fish at the mouth of the Amazon, a tree falls in the Adirondack wilderness, a man sneezes in Germany, a horse dies in Tartary, and twins are born in France. What does that mean? Does the contemporaneity of these events with one another, and with a million others as disjointed, form a rational bond between them, and unite them into anything that means for us a world? Yet just such a collateral contemporaneity, and nothing else, is the real order of the world. It is an order with which we have nothing to do but to get away from it as fast as possible. As

I said, we break it: we break it into histories, and we break it into arts, and we break it into sciences; and then we begin to feel at home. We make ten thousand separate serial orders of it, and on any one of these we react as though the others did not exist. We discover among its various parts relations that were never given to sense at all (mathematical relations, tangents, squares, and roots and logarithmic functions), and out of an infinite number of these we call certain ones essential and lawgiving, and ignore the rest. Essential these relations are, but only *for our purpose*, the other relations being just as real and present as they; and our purpose is to *conceive simply* and to *foresee*. Are not simple conception and prevision subjective ends pure and simple? They are the ends of what we call science; and the miracle of miracles, a miracle not yet exhaustively cleared up by any philosophy, is that the given order lends itself to the remodeling. It shows itself plastic to many of our scientific, to many of our aesthetic, to many of our practical purposes and ends.

When the man of affairs, the artist, or the man of science fails, he is not rebutted. He tries again. He says the impressions of sense *must* give way, *must* be reduced to the desiderated form. They all postulate in the interests of their volitional nature a harmony between the latter and the nature of things. The theologian does no more. And the reflex doctrine of the mind's structure, though all theology should as yet have failed of its endeavor, could but confess that the endeavor itself at least obeyed in form the mind's most necessary law.

# A. N. WHITEHEAD

## 2: The Organization of Thought

*In the following paragraphs, A. N. Whitehead asks and answers a key question: What is the actual world? It is a continuum; it is a mess. Our awareness of uniformity in the world of experience is an awareness that comes from ourselves, not directly from the* disjecta membra *that make up our moment-to-moment sense experience. "The creation of the world is the first unconscious act of speculative thought." Whitehead asks how we do this creating, how our "thought" applies to the* continua *of experience. It is a question we are still asking. These two excerpts, from speeches delivered in 1915 and 1916, may be taken, then, as developing James's description of "the world's contents" and the mysterious relation of that world to the verbal activity that purports to express it.*

*Like James, Whitehead combined a career in science (in this case mathematics) with a career in philosophy. When these two speeches were made to academic scientific groups in England, he was a professor of mathematics at Imperial College of Science and Technology. It was not until 1924 that he came to Harvard to teach philosophy, where he remained for the rest of his very active and productive life.*

THE SUBJECT of this address is the organization of thought, a topic evidently capable of many diverse modes of treatment.

I intend more particularly to give some account of that department of logical science with which some of my own studies have been connected. But I am anxious, if I can succeed in so doing, to handle this account so as to exhibit the relation with certain considerations which underlie general scientific activities. . . .

First, there is one point which it is necessary to emphasize. There is a tendency in analyzing scientific processes to assume a given assemblage of concepts applying to nature, and to imagine that the discovery of laws of nature consists in selecting by means of inductive logic some one out of a definite set of possible alternative relations which may hold between the things in nature answering to these obvious concepts. In a sense this assumption is fairly correct, especially in regard to the earlier stages of science. Mankind found itself in possession of certain concepts respecting nature—for example, the concept of fairly permanent material bodies—and proceeded to determine laws which related the corresponding percepts in nature. But the formulation of laws changed the concepts, sometimes gently by an added precision, sometimes violently. At first this process was not much noticed or at least was felt to be a process curbed within narrow bounds, not touching fundamental ideas. At the stage where we now are, the formulation of the concepts can be seen to be as important as the formulation of the empirical laws connecting the events in the universe as thus conceived by us. For example, the concepts of life, of heredity, of a material body, of a molecule, of an atom, of an electron, of energy, of space, of time, of quantity, and of number. I am not dogmatizing about the best way of getting such ideas straight. Certainly it will only be done by those who have devoted themselves to a special study of the facts in question. Success is never absolute, and progress in the right direction is the result of a slow, gradual process of continual comparison of ideas with facts. The criterion of success is that we should be able to formulate empirical laws, that is, statements of relations, connecting the various parts of the universe as thus conceived, laws with the property that we can interpret the actual events of our lives as being our fragmentary knowledge of this conceived interrelated whole.

But, for the purpose of science, what is the actual world? Has science to wait for the termination of the metaphysical debate till it can determine its own subject matter? I suggest that science has a much more homely starting ground. Its task is the discovery of the relations which exist within that flux of perceptions, sensations, and emotions which forms our experience of life. The panorama yielded by sight, sound, taste, smell, touch, and by more inchoate sensible feelings, is the sole field of activity. It is in this way that science is the thought organization of experience. The most obvious aspect of this field of actual experience is its disorderly character. It is for each person a *continuum*, fragmentary, and with elements not clearly differentiated. The comparison of the sensible experiences of diverse people brings its own difficulties. I insist on the radically untidy, ill-adjusted character of the fields of actual experience from which science starts. To grasp this fundamental truth is the first step in wisdom, when constructing a philosophy of science. This fact is concealed by the influence of language, molded by science, which foists on us exact concepts as though they represented the immediate deliverances of experience. The result is, that we imagine that we have immediate experience of a world of perfectly defined objects implicated in perfectly defined events which, as known to us by the direct deliverance of our senses, happen at exact instants of time, in a space formed by exact points, without parts and without magnitude: the neat, trim, tidy, exact world which is the goal of scientific thought.

My contention is, that this world is a world of ideas, and that its internal relations are relations between abstract concepts, and that the elucidation of the precise connection between this world and the feelings of actual experience is the fundamental question of scientific philosophy. The question which I am inviting you to consider is this: How does exact thought apply to the fragmentary, vague *continua* of experience? I am not saying that it does not apply: quite the contrary. But I want to know how it applies. The solution I am asking for is not a phrase, however brilliant, but a solid branch of science, constructed with slow patience, showing in detail how the correspondence is effected. . . .

If I understand Kant rightly—which I admit to be very problematical—he holds that in the act of experience we are aware of space and time as ingredients necessary for the occurrence of experience. I would suggest—rather timidly—that this doctrine should be given a different twist, which in fact turns it in the opposite direction—namely, that in the act of experience we perceive a whole formed of related differentiated parts. The relations between these parts possess certain characteristics, and time and space are the expressions of some of the characteristics of these relations. Then the generality and uniformity which are ascribed to time and space express what may be termed the uniformity of the texture of experience.

The success of mankind—modest though it is—in deducing uniform laws of nature is, so far as it goes, a testimony that this uniformity of texture goes beyond those characteristics of the data of experience which are expressed as time and space. Time and space are necessary to experience in the sense that they are characteristics of our experience; and of course, no one can have our experience without running into them. I cannot see that Kant's deduction amounts to much more than saying that "what is, is"—true enough, but not very helpful.

But I admit that what I have termed the "uniformity of the texture of experience" is a most curious and arresting fact. I am quite ready to believe that it is a mere illusion; and later on in the paper I suggest that this uniformity does not belong to the immediate relations of the crude data of experience, but is the result of substituting for them more refined logical entities, such as relations between relations, or classes of relations, or classes of classes of relations. By this means it can be demonstrated—I think—that the uniformity which must be ascribed to experience is of a much more abstract attenuated character than is usually allowed. This process of lifting the uniform time and space of the physical world into the status of logical abstractions has also the advantage of recognizing another fact, namely, the extremely fragmentary nature of all direct individual conscious experience.

My point in this respect is that fragmentary individual experiences are all that we know, and that all speculation must start from these *disjecta membra* as its sole datum. It is not true that we are directly aware of a smooth running world, which in our speculations we are to conceive as given. In my view the creation of the world is the first unconscious act of speculative thought; and the first task of a self-conscious philosophy is to explain how it has been done. . . .

I emphasize the point that our only exact data as to the physical world are our sensible perceptions. We must not slip into the fallacy of assuming that we are comparing a given world with given perceptions of it. The physical world is, in some general sense of the term, a deduced concept.

Our problem is, in fact, to fit the world to our perceptions, and not our perceptions to the world.

JAMES B. CONANT

# 3: The Changing Scientific Scene 1900-1950

*With this third selection we confront a longer account of more recent scientific developments by an eminent contemporary scientist and public figure. The discrepancies noted by James and Whitehead, between the actual experience of our senses on the one hand and the man-made orderliness of language on the other, are now seen as relevant to even larger areas. The problem of how to "get straight," as Whitehead put it, such changing concepts as life, an atom, time, space, now become more pressing for scientists a generation later. In several significant fields of investigation, "a certain ambiguity has set in." The difficulties over defining the nature of light are especially pertinent to our concern with language. The layman persists in phrasing his innocent inquiry on an "either-or" basis. "Light must be either particles or waves—now which is it?" The scientist's answer, Conant tells us, has to be "That is not a useful question." The layman is left to ponder how many of the questions he daily asks in ordinary life may be called, for similar reasons, "not useful."*

*It is not true, Whitehead remarked, that we are directly aware of a smooth-running world; only in the deduced world of scientific thought do we find anything "neat, trim, tidy." Now it appears that even—or especially—in that deduced world, the tidiness (as Whitehead foresaw) is breaking down. The passages Conant quotes from P. W. Bridgman are particu-*

15

*larly alarming: "We are now approaching a bound beyond which we are forever estopped from pushing our inquiries, not by the construction of the world, but by the construction of ourselves. The world fades out and eludes us because it becomes meaningless." This is, perhaps, one scientist's brief indulgence in romantic agony, and certainly these sentiments would be disputed by many reputable colleagues, especially perhaps in branches of science other than physics. Nevertheless the reeling reader may apply such remarks again to his daily life, his own elusive world.*

*This passage reprints most of a Bampton Lecture delivered by Dr. Conant at Columbia University in 1952. In the following year he resigned as president of Harvard to become High Commissioner for Germany, and since then has made a well-publicized effort to improve education in American high schools, both in science and in the entire academic program.*

SCORES OF books and hundreds, perhaps thousands, of articles have been written in the last dozen years on a single topic that might be designated as "the philosophic implications of the recent revolution in physics." Yet I am inclined to think that the layman is far from clear as to what has occurred in physics that warrants the name of revolution; nor is he at all certain as to what the implications of modern science are for his own private hopes, fears, and ambitions. Indeed, even in the more rarefied atmosphere inhabited by mathematicians, logicians, epistemologists, and theoretical physicists there is far from complete agreement as to the relation of the concepts of modern physics to various world hypotheses that for generations have been the subject of speculation by philosophers. To the lay observer this much seems quite certain: something tremendously exciting has happened in the area we designate as physics; this something is a complex of unexpected experimental results obtained during the last fifty years together with startlingly new theoretical ideas that have been enormously fruitful. What has happened is only distantly related in terms of logic and history to the explosion of the first atomic bomb; yet to most people, including many scientists, the large-scale release of atomic energy accomplished since 1940 is a symbol of the new physics. A revolutionary weapon and the dream of a revolutionary future source of industrial power have become thoroughly entangled with what some believe to be a revolution in man's concept of the universe.

Of all the features of the changed scientific scene, the fact that matter can be annihilated seems to many nonscientists the most bizarre. The popular writers on this subject have let no occasion pass to emphasize that the destruction of Hiroshima was the consequence of the annihilation of a small amount of matter which was converted into the energy that laid waste a city. To some, the real disappearance of matter seems as disturbing as the loss of life and ruin of the city, for associated with the word "matter" in most people's minds is the word "reality." . . .

The interconversion of matter and energy will not be regarded by most physicists as the exciting part of what has occurred in the last thirty or forty years. Far more significant, they will say, is the new outlook as regards the nature of light and the quantitative formulation of its interaction with matter. For example, P. W. Bridgman has declared "that since the turn of the century the physicist has passed through what amounts to an intellectual crisis forced by the discovery of experimental facts of a sort which he had not previously envisaged, and which he would not even have thought possible." [1]

As Professor Bridgman's words make clear, we are concerned not with a spectacular advance in science, but apparently with a break in the continuity of a line of argumentation. It is fair to call what has occurred a revolution in scientific thought, for what has taken place is a changed attitude on the part of

[1] P. W. Bridgman, "Philosophical Implications of Physics," in American Academy of Arts and Sciences, *Bulletin*, Vol. III, No. 5 (February, 1950).

physicists. This change has been forced by a series of experimental findings that have confronted the scientist with a dilemma that would have been regarded as impossible seventy-five years ago. All this is quite different from a so-called revolutionary discovery like the discovery of radioactivity; it is more closely akin to the formulation of such epoch-making new concepts as those embodied in Newtonian mechanics or Darwin's theory of evolution. Yet some would probably maintain that the new physics is more of a revolution, represents more of a break with the past than has the introduction of any new theory in science since 1600. But in attempting to evaluate the lasting effect of a series of intellectual events, one must remember that, as a rule, an altered direction of thought appears more drastic to those who live through the period of transition than to their descendants. It is by no means clear how the revolution in physics of the first half of the twentieth century will be regarded by the historians of science in the twenty-first century.

To illustrate what seems to me the essence of the new departure in scientific thought, I am going to use an analogy. Let me ask you to consider not light, but heat, and to recall that somewhat more than a hundred years ago popular lecturers on science fascinated their audiences by demonstrating that heat was a "mode of motion." The notion of a subtle caloric fluid that flowed from hot bodies to cooler ones could be shown to be totally unnecessary; indeed, not only unnecessary but also quite incapable of accounting for a number of experimental results, such as the generation of heat by friction. Therefore, the caloric theory of heat which had been useful in its day was disproved and in its place was firmly established the concept that heat was associated with the motion of particles. Nevertheless, the caloric theory of heat has remained a useful pedagogic device. We still talk of the flow of heat and even set up mathematical expressions to formulate this flow as though there were a caloric fluid. Within a limited range of experimental facts in physics and chemistry, the caloric theory of heat is still the most convenient way of ordering these facts. Note that I said "limited range of facts," for it was the introduction of other experimental situations that destroyed the over-all usefulness of the notion of a caloric fluid. To retain this theory and yet account for all these new facts, one would have had to add arbitrary assumption to assumption. On the other hand, when the theory was discarded and heat formulated in terms of the motions of particles, a vast new set of possibilities opened up. In short, experiments settled conclusively, so we say, which one of two theories of heat was "true."

At the end of the last century the nature of light seemed to be as definitely settled as did the nature of heat. Light was an electromagnetic disturbance in all-pervading ether; it was a wave phenomenon. The older idea that light was corpuscular —a stream of bullets—had been destroyed, so it was said, by a certain set of famous experiments that proved that light was in fact undulatory. Then along came certain new experimental phenomena which were as difficult to fit into a wave theory of light as had been the older set to fit into the framework of the corpuscular theory. About 1910 a highly unsatisfactory situation had developed which could be summarized by saying that light is emitted and received as though it consisted of a stream of particles and it is transmitted as though it were a set of waves. To the scientists of forty years ago this was the equivalent of saying a box was both full and empty; it was impossible, so they maintained, for light to be both undulatory and corpuscular. The fact that this appeared to be the case could only be a temporary situation. It would surely be only a matter of time before a set of experiments would be devised that would resolve the difficulty, for such a sequence of events had occurred throughout the history of science.

One is tempted to say that what has happened in the last forty years is that physicists have learned to love a situation they once thought to be intolerable. It is as though their predecessors had been forced to retain the caloric fluid not only as a matter of convenience in formulating certain experiments, but also as a matter of necessity, and yet the evidence against the theory remained unshaken. Furthermore, it is as though their predecessors had decided that the very nature of energy and matter was such that it was impossible to decide for or against the two ideas of heat: the caloric theory or heat as a mode of motion. But such a decision on the part of early-nineteenth-century scientists would have been a negation of science itself—at least, so people would have declared until very recent years. The progress of science consisted in testing the deductions from various hypotheses and discarding the hypothesis the deductions from which were contradicted by experiment. The idea that there could be two diametrically opposed theories as to the nature of heat, or of light, or of matter, and that both could be rejected and confirmed as a consequence of experiments would have been considered nonsense to almost all sane people fifty years ago. In regard to heat we can still agree that the caloric fluid is obsolete, make no mistake about that; in regard to light, however, we can hardly do better than say that light is in a sense both undulatory and corpuscular. In regard to matter, we have already seen that here too a certain ambiguity has entered in. . . .

One of the prime factors in changing the scientific point of view has been the failure to settle by experiment the validity of the wave theory versus the corpuscular theory of light. I have suggested earlier that the physicist has learned to live with a paradox that once seemed intolerable. It might be better to say that he has discovered how general is the paradox and by what mathematical manipulations of experimental data he can get forward with all manner of undertakings because of the paradox. If a layman persists today with the question: is a beam of light composed of particles or waves, he would probably receive an answer from most philosophically minded physicists somewhat as follows: "That is not a useful question. We physicists have stopped asking it; but if you insist, we may say that a beam of light is at one and the same time a set of particles and waves. But let us hasten to add, so is a beam of electrons or of rapidly moving atomic nuclei. Furthermore, lest you confuse the new physics with the mere failure of the old, let me make it plain that in our new conceptual scheme we can define mathematically our uncertainties as to the interaction of a stream of particles or waves with larger aggregates of matter. In short, there is a whole new branch of physics called quantum mechanics that now accommodates a vast amount of experimental material in both physics and chemistry and has been as fruitful as any development in the history of the physical sciences. So if the solidity of matter seems to have gone out from under you, don't for a moment think that this has impeded the advance of science, for quite the contrary is the case." . . .

Just what does the new outlook mean for those interested in constructing a total picture of the universe? Professor Bridgman has said, in considering the philosophical implications of physics:

"Finally, I come to what it seems to me may well be from the long range point of view the most revolutionary of the insights to be derived from our recent experiences in physics, more revolutionary than the insights afforded by the discoveries of Galileo and Newton, or of Darwin. This is the insight that it is impossible to transcend the human reference point. . . . The new insight comes from a realization that the structure of nature may eventually be such that our processes of thought do not correspond to it sufficiently to permit us to think about it at all. We have already had an intimation of this in the behavior of very small things in the quantum domain . . . there can be no difference of opinion with regard to the dilemma that now confronts us in the direction of the very small. We are now approaching a bound beyond which we are forever estopped from pushing our inquiries, not by the construction of the world, but by the construction of ourselves. The world fades out and eludes us because it becomes meaningless. We cannot even express this in the way we would like. We cannot say that there exists a world beyond any knowl-

edge possible to us because of the nature of knowledge. The
very concept of existence becomes meaningless. It is literally
true that the only way of reacting to this is to shut up. We are
confronted with something truly ineffable. We have reached
the limit of the vision of the great pioneers of science,
the vision, namely that we live in a sympathetic world, in that
it is comprehensible by our minds." [2]

Professor Dingle of London has written, "The men who
carried on the scientific tradition established in the seventeenth century did so truly and faithfully, but thinking all
the time that they were doing something else. The revolution
that came in the twentieth century was simply the overthrow
of the false notion of what science was and is; science itself
has pursued the same undeviating course from Galileo through
Newton and Einstein to our own time." [3]

"What the mid-nineteenth-century scientists thought they
were doing," Dingle goes on to say, was looking out "upon a
real external substantial world of material bodies whose content was measured by its mass or weight. . . . The information thus provided gave clues—often very indirect—to the
eternal and unchanging principles that were firmly believed
to underlie the behavior of the world. . . .

The world was thus regarded as exhibiting, with the passage of time, a succession of states, each connected with its
predecessor and successor by what were regarded as unbreak-
able links of absolute necessity. This was referred to as the
principle of cause and effect. . . .

"In general terms we may say that the Victorians looked
on the progress of science as a process of accumulation. . . .
Our view today is very different . . . the picture of the
whole which we form in our attempt to express its interrelations undergoes unceasing transformations. . . . We can no
longer say, The World is like this, or the World is like that.

[2] Ibid.
[3] Herbert Dingle, "The Scientific Outlook in 1851 and in 1951," British
Journal for the Philosophy of Science, II (1951), 86.

We can only say, Our experience up to the present is best represented by a world of this character; I do not know what model will best represent the world of tomorrow, but I do know that it will co-ordinate a greater range of experience than that of today." [4]

According to this interpretation of the history of science, what nineteenth-century physicists thought they were doing was discovering the causal laws that governed the world of material substance; actually, to use Professor Dingle's words, "They were at little more than the beginning of their task of understanding the world of experience." Yet in contrasting the present with the past, it is important to note that not all nineteenth-century scientists were of one mind as to the nature of their task. One need only mention the name of Ernst Mach, whose point of view in our own time has led to the doctrines of the logical empiricists, to indicate that there were some skeptics in regard to the possibilities of determining once and for all the nature of the material universe. P. G. Tait in 1876 in his lectures on "Some Recent Advances in Physical Science" stated that "nothing is more preposterously unscientific than to assert (as is constantly done by the quasi-scientific writers of the present day) that with the utmost strides attempted by science we should necessarily be sensibly nearer to a conception of the ultimate nature of matter." Even as orthodox a physicist as J. J. Thomson reflected the same view when, in the introductory paragraphs to his little book *The Corpuscular Theory of Matter*, published in 1907, he stated that his new theory was not to be regarded as "an ultimate one; its object is physical," he said, "rather than metaphysical." And he added these significant words, "From the point of view of the physicist, a theory of matter is a policy rather than a creed; its object is to connect or co-ordinate apparently diverse phenomena and above all to suggest, stimulate, and direct experiment."

If I tried to sum up in a sentence what seems to me

[4] *Ibid.*, pp. 89, 98-99.

the philosophic implications of the new physics, I should be inclined to paraphrase Sir J. J. Thomson. A mass of experimental evidence in the twentieth century has provided powerful ammunition to those who look upon a scientific theory as a policy and has made untenable at least one theory regarded as a creed. A policy suggests always a guide to action, and of the various interpretations of science that are current today, those seem to me to be the most useful that emphasize the dynamic nature of science. There are philosophers, I realize, who draw a sharp line between knowing and doing and look askance at all philosophizing that seems to tie the search for truth in any way to practical undertakings. But for me, at least, any analysis of the process of testing a statement made in a scientific context leads at once to a series of actions. Therefore, I venture to define science as a series of interconnected concepts and conceptual schemes arising from experiment and observation and fruitful of further experiments and observations. The test of a scientific theory is, I suggest, its fruitfulness—in the words of Sir J. J. Thomson, its ability "to suggest, stimulate, and direct experiment."

The fallacy underlying what some might call the eighteenth and nineteenth century misconceptions of the nature of scientific investigations seems to lie in a mistaken analogy. Those who said they were investigating the structure of the universe imagined themselves as the equivalent of the early explorers and map makers. The explorers of the fifteenth and sixteenth centuries had opened up new worlds with the aid of imperfect maps; in their accounts of distant lands, there had been some false and many ambiguous statements. But by the time everyone came to believe the world was round, the maps of distant continents were beginning to assume a fairly consistent pattern. By the seventeenth century, methods of measuring space and time had laid the foundations for an accurate geography. The increased success of empirical procedures in improving the work of artisans was already improving men's accuracy of observation. Therefore, by a series of successive approximations, so to speak, maps and descriptions of distant lands were becoming closer and closer to accurate accounts of reality. Why would not the labors of those who worked in laboratories have the same outcome? No one doubted that there were real rivers, mountains, trees, bays with tides, rainfall, snowfall, glaciers; one could doubt any particular map or description, of course, but given time and patience, it was assumed the truth would be ascertained. By the same token there must be a truth about the nature of heat, light, and matter.

To be sure, the map makers had been observing gross objects like rocks and trees, rivers and mountains, while, as science progressed, the force of gravity and atoms and waves in the ether became the preoccupation of the physicist. Still, tentative ideas played a similar part in both enterprises; working hypotheses as to the nature of a river valley, the source of a lake, or the frontier of a mountain range seemed to be the equivalent of the caloric fluid or the early corpuscular theory of light. The early geographers' methods of identification were essentially those of common sense. Any given set of observations might be in error. Yet even erroneous assumptions might serve, at times, a useful purpose. To have assumed the existence of a lake beyond a certain mountain range might prove fortunate; as a "working hypothesis," even if false, it might lead an explorer to important goals.

Of course, the possibility of error exists in all surveys. Indeed, one can image a situation where even in geography no final certainty is possible. Assume an island surrounded by reefs that make direct access out of the question except with special equipment, and assume an explorer without such equipment. He must content himself for the time being with telescopic observations from several angles; he can thus construct a map but with many uncertainties. For example, are those highly colored areas due to rocks or to vegetation? On his return with adequate equipment, he can land, go to the colored areas and directly determine their composition. If before he returns, the island disappears below the surface of the ocean, that makes no difference as to the validity of his methods. We are all sure that in principle he could have returned and determined the accuracy of his suppositions about the nature of the terrain.

This use of the "in principle" argument, I have already pointed out, was the basis for the nineteenth-century physicist's confidence in his picture of a gas with its rapidly moving particles. Those who still hold today with the idea that the universe has a structure which, like the geography of an island, can be discovered by successive approximations, must cling to the "in principle" argument. Confront them with the phlogiston theory, the caloric fluid, the luminiferous ether— all now obsolete (except for pedagogic purposes)—and they will say, "Yes, the first maps were imperfect, but in principle it is possible to find out what really is the structure of the universe."

On this basic issue there is far from complete agreement among philosophers of science today. You can, each of you, choose your side and find highly distinguished advocates for the point of view you have selected. However, in view of the revolution in physics, anyone who now asserts that science is an exploration of the universe must be prepared to shoulder a heavy burden of proof. To my mind, the analogy between the map maker and the scientist is false. A scientific theory is not even the first approximation to a map; it is not a creed; it is a policy—an economical and fruitful guide to action by scientific investigators.

But lest my skepticism distort the picture unduly, let me point out how little the new physics has altered some of the older conceptual schemes of physics and chemistry; let me emphasize what an excellent policy the new physics has proved to be in terms of experiments. What disturbs many people are the difficulties that arise if we accept the map-maker analogy. That two conceptual schemes should appear so dissimilar as the wave formulation of the laws governing the transmission of light, on the one hand, and the corpuscular theory of light emission, on the other, distresses those who have looked to the physical sciences for an ever increasing degree of explanation as to how matter is "really constructed." It almost seems as though the modern physicist were like an explorer who, uncertain as to whether the colored areas dimly seen from a distance were rocks or trees, found on landing they were both! But this is a false parallel; it would be far better to say that the physicist seems now to be in the position of an explorer who can never land on the distant island. In short, the whole analogy between a map and a scientific theory is without a basis.

One objection to the point of view I am advocating in these lectures may be considered briefly at this point. It is to the effect that if a scientific theory is not even an approximation to a map of a portion of the universe, the so-called advance of pure science is nothing but a game; from which it would follow, so the objection runs, that the justification of science is to be found only in the application of science to the practical arts. The answer to those who put forward arguments of this type is to remind them of the work of mathematicians, painters, poets, and musical composers. To my mind, the significance of the fabric of scientific theories that have been produced in the last three hundred and fifty years is the same as the significance of the art of the great periods in history, or the significance of the work of the musical composers. For most scientists, I think the justification of their work is to be found in the pure joy of its creativeness; the spirit which moves them is closely akin to the imaginative vision which inspires an artist. To some degree, almost all men today applaud the success of the past in the realm of creative work and do not measure the degree of success by material standards. So too, at some distant time, the advance of science from 1600 to 1950 may be regarded entirely as a triumph of

the creative spirit, one manifestation of those vast poten-
tialities of men and women that make us all proud to be members of the human race.

A second objection to the skepticism of those of us who
regard all scientific theories as formulations of policy is that
our view is only a transitory social phenomenon. One must
admit that perhaps the children now in elementary school
may in the middle life feel that a picture of the universe that
seems no picture is quite a satisfactory model. To be sure, it
took generations for people to become accustomed to the concept of a force of gravity acting at a distance without any
medium to transmit the force. Certainly by the year 2052,
relativity and quantum mechanics will occupy a different position in the total science of that day from that assigned to them
at present. When these new ideas have been assimilated into
the culture of the times, the idea of science as an inquiry into
the structure of the universe may once again become firmly
established in people's minds.

My bet as to the future, however, is on the other horse. It
seems to me more likely that the average citizen will come
to think of science in totally different terms from those employed in explaining science to lay audiences fifty years ago.
If I am right, in order to assimilate science into the culture of
our twentieth-century highly industrialized society, we must
regard scientific theories as guides to human action and thus
an extension of common sense. At all events, this is the point
of view presented in these lectures.

# HERBERT J. MULLER

## 4: A Note on Methods of Analysis

*In this passage we begin to face more closely some relations
between new science and new uses of language. The passage is
taken from a book called* Science and Criticism, *written by a
student of the humanities who is concerned with relating attitudes of modern science with aesthetic attitudes, particularly
those of literary criticism. The "either-or" fallacy, attacked
by Conant in his review of the physicists' problems with light,
becomes here more widely described as "the unconditional behavior of the dogmatist" and "in a real sense pathological." In
the conditions of "complexity, relativity, multiplicity, flux"
that science has given us, this author calls for a "lithe, sinuous,
athletic type of mind" capable of constant readjustment. The
whole passage is, among other things, an appeal to express
oneself in terms of degrees rather than in terms of sheep-or-
goats, in daily life as well as in academic or literary matters.*

*Herbert J. Muller is not to be confused with Hermann
Joseph Muller, the Nobel prize-winning zoologist, even though
both men are associated with Indiana University. Herbert J.
Muller is a distinguished professor of English who has written
widely on science and history as well. His latest book,* Freedom
in the Ancient World, *appeared in 1961.*

EMERSON REMARKED that it is a good thing, now and then, to take a look at the landscape from between one's legs. Although this stunt might seem pointless when things are already topsy-turvy, it can be the more helpful then. One may say that what this chaotic world needs first of all is more *disso*ciation; by breaking up factitious alliances and oppositions, one may get at the deep uniformities. Or what this nightmarish world needs is the strategy of the dream, which appears to multiply and magnify contradictions but actually ignores them. ("Dreams are particularly fond of reducing antitheses to uniformity," Freud wrote, "or representing them as one and the same thing.") Specifically, the situation calls for a technique of analysis that Kenneth Burke names "perspective by incongruity."

In its simplest form, this is merely a violation of the intellectual proprieties by mating words that have moved in different circles—as when Mencken described hygiene as "medicine made corrupt by morality." Such bundlings are the essence of paradox and epigram, and a familiar trick of humorists and satirists. They are also the essence of metaphor. And as a marking of unsuspected connections they lead, ultimately, to the heart of all thought and knowledge. The great revolutionary thinkers are those who most violently wrenched traditional associations; Karl Marx was a philosophical Oscar Wilde, more scandalous because more sober. Hence Burke has deliberately, systematically cultivated "the methodology of the pun." Throughout *Attitudes toward History* he uses the religious vocabulary of motives for describing aesthetic and practical activities, the aesthetic for religious and practical, the practical for religious and aesthetic. By such impious means he piously strives to integrate these vital interests. Perspective by incongruity enables the perception of essential congruity.

The lead here is the parable of the pike. Placed in a tank with some minnows but separated from them by a sheet of glass, the pike bangs its head for some time in an effort to get at them. At length it sensibly gives up the effort. Much less sensibly, it continues to ignore the minnows after the glass is removed; it fails to revaluate the situation. In other words, it becomes a dogmatist. For just so are men's powers of analysis and adaptation stupefied by unconditional, is-nothing-but generalizations. Thinkers demand that we choose naturalism *or* idealism, communism *or* capitalism, revolution *or* reaction. In the name of realism they copy the pike.

This approach admittedly offers an easy way of calling people names, and may become merely the sport of an intellectual playboy. Nevertheless the unconditional behavior of the dogmatist is in a real sense pathological. Freud has made us aware of the dynamic, reflex relation between emotion and symbol or idea. These reflexes are up to a point socially necessary; communal effort demands a certain measure of identification, personification, or downright symbolic fraud. The difficulty, however, lies in locating the point and determining the measure. Given the impossibility of general agreement upon what are the "right" ideas or how much emotion is "normal," their intimacy is plainly a hazard. In any event an unalterable association is the sign of the fanatic, ultimately of the lunatic. And here is a clue to the extreme nervous tension in the modern world. Psychologists have been inducing nervous breakdowns in animals by stepping up the demands upon their powers of adjustment and suddenly reversing signals to which they have become conditioned; under such artificial stress the animal becomes jittery and finally goes to pieces. Similarly men break down in a rapidly changing world that demands constant readjustment. Yet these demands need not be so intolerable a strain. Men can maintain efficient reserves, they are naturally flexible, they are physiologically capable of far more extensive readjustment. Only by permitting themselves to become absolutely conditioned to some expectation do they become unequal to shifting demands. There is occasion enough today for viewing with alarm; nevertheless men themselves create the occasion and cultivate the habit of alarm.

The method of "planned incongruity" can accordingly be a practical, social way of making men at home in the world they perforce have to live in. As Burke says, it is a way of making perspectives *"cheap and easy."* There is some real cheapening of quality, indeed; uncompromising devotion to a creed is also a form of virtue and strength. But the gain in efficiency and practical wisdom more than compensates for the loss. Complexity, relativity, multiplicity, flux—the conditions of modern experience cannot be liquidated by any effort of thought or legislative degree. They call for a lithe, sinuous, athletic type of mind. The thinkers who bulge with muscular dogma are like the strong men of the advertisements, very impressive, but a little monstrous; and at that they are no match for gorillas like Goering.

I do not propose to employ this method as systematically—or self-consciously—as Burke. But it is manifestly pertinent to my main intention, of relating scientific and literary meanings and bringing them both back to the public world. More specifically, it will be a means of becoming oriented to modern science. Science always seems a little strange to the layman because in a sense it reverses the common notion of how we come to understand; it replaces the familiar particulars with increasingly unfamiliar abstractions—it explains the *known* in terms of the *unknown*. Modern physics in particular might be considered the most radical perspective by incongruity in the history of thought, for it has resulted from a deliberate violation of the axiomatic or self-evident, a methodical thinking of the unthinkable. And this brings up the ruling logic of modern science.

Bacon remarked the paradox that the term "ancient," with its connotations of mellow wisdom, is habitually applied to the *young* peoples in the history of the race. Actually we are the ancients, the Greeks were the precocious youngsters. Yet contemporaries are still inclined to obey these youngsters, as Dewey has taken pains to demonstrate. However unconsciously, they cling to the Greek concept of fixed forms or or eternal essences, by which variety, particularity, change, contingency—all that is most plainly given in direct experience—are made to seem like "mere" appearances, or accidents to be put up with. With this concept of Being they inherit a worry over ultimate Being—what makes action act, or causation cause, or being be. Above all, they still regard Aristotelian logic as the final arbiter of Truth. They subordinate to it the method of scientific inquiry, certainly the most efficient means to truth that man has yet devised. And the working logic of science is not only significantly different but in some ways inconsistent with the ancient canons.[1]

Bacon also remarked that Aristotle's logic is not subtle enough to deal with nature. For example, it cannot handle satisfactorily the quantitative relations that are fundamental for science. Its subject-predicate propositions have become more inadequate with the complex, multiple interrelations stressed in the important concept of organism. Its law of the excluded middle—a thing is either A or not-A—has recently come in for

[1] Since my references to Aristotle will usually be uncomplimentary, I wish to anticipate the charges of cocky modernism or professional irreverence. In a historical study, full justice could be done to his pioneering achievement, his whole important contribution to the life of reason and reasonableness. This, however, is a critical study of the present, its knowledge and needs. Aristotle's thought is a great monument; but the trouble with monuments, as Bacon said, is that they can only be celebrated, they cannot be moved or advanced. His basic principles—which are still religiously taught by disciples in our great universities—have made possible no considerable discovery, can generate no new knowledge. Dewey points out, moreover, that the very realism that distinguishes him from Plato has made him a more positive hindrance. He was primarily a student of the facts of nature, the wordly rather than the other-worldly, and he put the Platonic Ideas or eternal forms of Being back into nature. Here, after two thousand years, Darwin finally exploded them; but meanwhile Aristotle's basic assumptions had got into science, where they were unrecognized even by the seventeenth-century pioneers who believed that they had done with him, and they hampered its advance until Einstein. Altogether, our job is to do for our age what Aristotle so brilliantly did for his. We can hope to succeed only by recognizing that thought is a historical enterprise, not a final solution.

especial attack. Although this law is up to a point a necessity of thought, strictly it is refuted by life itself; a living organism, always growing and changing, is at every moment itself and something else, and demands as well a law of the *included* middle: a thing may be *both* A and not-A.[2] In general, criticism centers on Aristotle's static, absolute, immutabel categories. In their practice, at least, scientists observe no such categories. They employ an instrumental logic that controls inquiry but is also controlled by inquiry; they will break any law of thought in order to make a law of nature.

Modern philosophers, accordingly, no longer recognize one fixed, essential logic but are developing a number of logics, including notably one of relations. The intricacies and refinements of these systems are beyond the scope of my present purposes, not to say my attainments. For the moment a simplified version of the new techniques of thinking will do well enough; and such a one is the "dynamic logic" outlined by Boris B. Bogoslovsky in *The Technique of Controversy*. He states four main principles: (1) A must never be used without not-A. The statement that all men are selfish has no useful meaning—or if taken literally, as by the youthful cynic, is seriously misleading—unless we state that men are also unselfish. (2) The references of a word must be explicit. "Selfishness" has various aspects and implications, and confusion is inevitable until we specify the meaning we have in mind. (3) The assumption of continuity and interaction demands the principle of "bothness." Thinkers have long debated such questions as whether men are products of heredity

---

[2] Zeno's famous sophisms are a case in point. His problem of just how many hairs are needed to make a beard, how many grains of sand to make a heap, is a real problem—*if* we hold that there be either beard or no beard, heap or no heap. The problem disappears the moment we take our minds off mere words and consider natural facts. Similarly Zeno's demonstration that Achilles cannot overtake a tortoise has bothered philosophers for centuries, even though Achilles always can catch the tortoise, because it is logical by the old canons. What the paradox actually demonstrates is that this logic cannot handle continuous change.

or of environment; obviously men are products of both, and thought must always take into account the continuous process, the inseparable conjunction. Hence (4) quantitative values must be made explicit. We must state *to what extent* a thing is A and not-A (selfish and unselfish), place it on the scale between these poles. Altogether, the aim of "dynamic logic" is sharper specification among multiple relations, more accurate location on a continuous scale. It is never independent of natural knowledge. It can spot the obvious fallacies resulting from reasoning by analogy; it nevertheless recognizes that given a world in which there are no absolute identities, *all* reasoning is by analogy.

Now this is indeed a simplified version of scientific logic, and as outlined will hardly seem revolutionary. Bogoslovsky makes it seem too easy, moreover, especially in his call for quantitative values. Long ago Hume pointed out the inevitable ambiguity in controversies over the degrees of a quality or circumstance; in the issues of the arts and humanities we cannot hope for utterly precise locations and measurements. Yet merely to recognize and define the problem is a considerable gain. Everything is indeed a matter of degree. For the practical purposes of thought it is not all one, as we say; it is always two. If we mark the poles, include the middle, use a sliding scale, we can at least hope to make controversy more profitable; ideas may approach and not merely collide like billiard balls. The assertion that the Heart sees farther than the Head gets us nowhere, until we specify what kind of thing it sees better, under what circumstances, for what purposes— always remembering that heart and head see in conjunction, and are not engaged in a seeing contest. And elementary as these principles may seem, few thinkers consistently apply them. The logic of most discourse is still based on the sheep-or-goat concept of truth.

Thus critics tend to treat as independent, exclusive principles such poles as romanticism and classicism, freedom and tradition, form and substance, dogma and sensibility, individualism and collectivism, self-expression and communication—head and tail. They snap continuities by the use of "versus," making antitheses of complementary principles that are at work in all artists at all times; they take a stand at one end of a scale as if it were the norm, the absolute A of beauty or truth; they make out degrees only in terms of error or evil. They then erect policies into proverbs and proverbs into categorical laws. In effect they demand that we choose between the principle that one should look before he leaps and the principle that he who hesitates is lost. An efficient logic should help us to tell when to leap and when to hesitate, enable us to keep clear of the leaping school and the hesitating school.

All this still amounts to a restatement of a general attitude rather than the formulation of a rigorous program. More often than not it will appear as a demonstration of platitudes, as that the same thing can always be at once good and bad. But through "planned incongruity" and the principle of ambivalence or polarity, one may set platitudes in a richer context, restore the living truth in truism, at times even startle. One may locate the good in the bad and the bad in the good, and then make for better. Thus regionalism in literature (to return to an illustration I have used elsewhere) appears as a relatively simple adaptation to life, a return to the old meanings of the family, the home, the soil. It may therefore be stigmatized as an evasion of the problem of assimilating the complex material of modern life, a shirking of responsibility, an escape. But it also may be applauded as a return to the grass roots of art and life, a recovery of essential pieties, a means of steadying a confused generation. Reviewers tend to use consistently either the "bad" or the "good" description; they speak kindly even of the feeble exhibits or coldly even of the sturdy ones. The ideal critic would command the whole scale of motives and values in regionalism and place a given work accordingly.

In these terms, at any rate, humanism is an effort to place

all doctrine on an appropriate scale, to see it in relation and in degree instead of as isolate truth or vagrant error, to provide a perspective in which dualistic aspects may again be seen as aspects of a whole—the organic whole that is the included middle. The yes and no constantly asserted in daily behavior are naturally translated into right and wrong, good and bad; but we can make choices without becoming Manichaeans.

P. W. BRIDGMAN

# 5: The Way Things Are

*This passage reprints the Introduction (with one or two minor omissions) of a recent book by the late physicist, P. W. Bridgman. Some of his earlier statements were quoted at length by Conant in our third selection, and what he says here should make better sense in the light of both Conant and Muller. Bridgman proceeds from his experience of the quantum theory and its emphasis on the observer to the conviction that only "the first person singular" faithfully expresses what man can express. His statement that "a system dealing with itself" leads to maladjustment might be compared with Muller's observation that dogmatism is pathological. Similarly, his account of the Ames-Cantril demonstrations might be accepted as a first-class instance of Muller's "perspective by incongruity." In any case here is a personal report from a leading scientist which suggests the state of mind of a man who has lived through the developments that Conant and Muller have been discussing. As always, the reader is urged to consult the entire book to see these suggestions worked out in detail, and he is reminded, once again, that the attitudes expressed here are those of one scientist, and not necessarily those of Science at large.*

*P. W. Bridgman spent his entire active life at Harvard, winning the Nobel Prize in physics for his work in high pressures in 1946. The book from which this Introduction is taken, a kind of scientific-philosophical-autobiographical summation*

THE WAY THINGS ARE       39

*called* The Way Things Are, *was published in 1959, two years before he died.*

THE NEW insights for which I am trying to find a place have mostly been suggested by recent experiences in science which I believe have revolutionary implications not appreciated even by most scientists. Two convictions have been growing upon me—a conviction of the importance of a better understanding of the nature and the limitations of our intellectual tools, and a conviction that there is some fundamental ineptness in the way that all of us handle our minds. It becomes more and more impossible for me to read any of the great philosophical writings which have excited universal admiration from the time of the early Greeks—my mind simply will not do the things that it is obviously expected to do. The recent *Treasury of Philosophy* of Dagobert Runes is to me an utterly depressing exhibition of human frailty. At the same time, the importance of putting my finger on what is the matter appears more and more pressing.

In some of my early writings I spoke of the twofold aspect of the problem of understanding—there was the problem of understanding the world around us, and there was the problem of understanding the process of understanding, that is, the problem of understanding the nature of the intellectual tools with which we attempt to understand the world around us. The implication in my early writings was that the latter is a closed problem which we may hope to solve now to a sufficient approximation, if for no other reason than that we have our minds with us for study and presumably could describe them exhaustively in terms presently in our control, whereas we must always be prepared for the discovery, by yet unknown techniques, of at present unknown structure within the present ultimate particles of physics or beyond the present universe of galaxies. Now this position may still be correct "in principle," although I am beginning to have my doubts. However, it is becoming more and more obvious that the problem of understanding the nature of our intellectual tools offers so many present complexities that it is not profitable to separate the one problem from the other in the way I did. In fact, the problem of better understanding our intellectual tools would at present seem to have priority. Even in pure physics, where the problem does not obtrude itself prominently, it is becoming evident that the problem of the "observer" must eventually deal with the observer as thinking about what he observes. In psychology, as a consequence of recent concern with analysis of brain activity in terms of machine activity, stimulated by the development of super-calculating machines, the problem of understanding the nature of the nervous apparatus with which we understand appears more unavoidable and more formidable. Eventually, when we understand better our intellectual tools, we may perhaps be able to put our finger on what is the matter with human thinking.

Any new insights which I may have been acquiring over the years cannot be dissociated from my constant practice of "operational analysis," which continually reveals itself as a fruitful line of attack. But much remains to be done, and I believe that some of even the more obvious implications of the operational approach have not yet been adequately explored, in particular, the fact that operations are performed by individuals. At the same time, the operational attitude appears as a special case of a more general attitude. It is evident, as its critics have often pointed out and I myself have repeatedly stated, that the operational approach cannot be completely general and that it can by no means provide the basis for a complete philosophy. There are many fundamental questions to be answered, such, for example, as: "What is an operation? On what basis is an operation accepted, or what makes an operation 'good'?" Some of the implications of this incompleteness I have explicitly recognized, as when I have tried to analyze operations into "instrumental" and "mental" or "verbal" and "paper-and-pencil" operations. Or, still more generally, when I have recognized a general and a particular aspect of operations, the particular aspects being those of primary concern to the physicist or other specialist, while the general aspects may be so general that from one point of view they degenerate into tautology. In general, an operational analysis appears as a particular case of an analysis in terms of activities—doings or happenings. In my own case, pursuit of operational analysis has resulted in the conviction, a conviction which has increased with the practice, that it is better to analyze in terms of doings or happenings than in terms of objects or static abstractions. Many professional philosophers will doubtless object that this begs the whole question, for it assumes that an analysis in terms of doings or happenings is possible. Whether this objection is valid in any ultimate sense we leave unexplored, at least for the present, but I believe that it is nevertheless possible to analyze at a level where the immediate emphasis is on doings or happenings, a thesis for which the existence of this book may be taken as partial justification. Furthermore, I believe it is a sort of analysis which everyone can learn to make, by observation of other practitioners if by no other method. Whether it is a more profitable method of analysis than an analysis in terms of things or other static elements can be judged only by the event. For myself I can only report that it puts nearly everything in a different and a fresher light.

Analyzing the world in terms of doings or happenings, as contrasted with analyzing in terms of things or static elements, amounts to doing something new and unusual. I believe that history shows that, whenever human beings find how to do something new, new vistas open. Seeking to discover the consequences of the new doing constitutes an exploration of discovery, the results of which may not be anticipated. This book may be regarded in the light of one of the many possible expeditions of exploration. We cannot tell until we go whether the results the expedition brings back will prove to be important. But even if the results are disappointing, there is still a certain intrinsic interest in finding out something about the nature of the unknown territory.

It was my original intention to present my analysis of doings or happenings exclusively in the first person singular, the doings or happenings being doings by me or happenings to me. My reason for this was, among others, my desire to secure the greatest possible immediacy in description, coupled with a conviction that an essential preliminary to successful analysis is faithful description.

The resolution to use the first person was one of the outcomes of the attempt to see things in terms of activities. A spoken or a written word was spoken or written by someone, and part of the recognition of the word as activity is a recognition of who it was that said it or wrote it. When I make a statement, even as coldly and impersonal a statement as a proposition of Euclid, it is I that am making the statement, and the fact that it is I that am making the statement is part of the picture of the activity. In the same way, when you quote a proposition of Euclid the fact that it is you who quote it is part of the picture which is not to be discarded. And when I quote you it is I that am doing the quoting. Attention to the activity aspect of all our communication inevitably forces mention of the maker of the communication, and in this book it is I that am making the communication.

My feeling of the desirability of giving my analysis in the first person has been with me for a long time, and I have in the past not infrequently used first person report and have even argued to justify it. This argument, and related arguments, I feel have to a large extent been misunderstood, and criticisms of my writings have frequently accused me of solipsism. These criticisms have always puzzled me. However, it is only recently that I have come to appreciate that use of the first person, which is all that I am urging, need involve no commitment whatever with regard to a solipsistic "ego" or "self," the implied existence of which is what I suppose has principally disturbed the critics. My use of the first person in reporting has the neutrality of grammar. That it can have such neutrality I regard as an important observation.

A program of first person report can be carried through by anyone, without prejudice. It is a matter of observation that people can talk to each other, each in his own first person. When my neighbor talks to me in his first person I understand what he is saying, and I take it that my neighbor understands what I mean when I talk to him in my first person.

So much for my original intentions and the justification for them. When it actually came to carrying through the program, however, situations frequently arose in which the urge to use the conventional impersonal manner of speech was strong and use of the first person appeared forced and clumsy. Instead of saying "I see that it is true that—," or even "We see that it is true that—," it is simpler, and, with our linguistic background, almost irresistible to say "It is true that—." I shall therefore not always hold my exposition explicitly to the first person. However, I, and I hope my reader, will be vividly aware that translation into the first person singular is always possible and implicit. When I say "we," I am speaking for myself and, I believe, also for you. That is, I believe that you might be uttering the same words as I. When I speak in impersonal general terms in the third person, this is a compressed way of saying "This is what I would say and I believe it is also what you would say." The question how it comes about that you and I can use the same words in similar situations we may leave for possible future analysis. For the present it is sufficient merely to call attention to the similarity in the brains and nervous systems of all of us, and to the similarities in much of our experience and environment.

In the following, the extent to which I find it desirable explicitly to use the first person will depend to a large extent on the subject matter. In discussing situations in physics or mathematics or any physical science, use of the third person is natural and usually adequate, but when it comes to situations involving a large social element, it seems to me that use of the first person becomes increasingly desirable, and indeed even necessary, if we are going to bring out into the light features usually ignored.

Insistence on the use of the first person, either explicitly or implicitly, will inevitably focus attention on the individual. This, it seems to me, is all to the good. The philosophical and scientific exposition of our age has been too much obsessed with the ideal of a coldly impersonal generality. This has been especially true of some mathematicians, who in their final publications carefully erase all trace of the scaffolding by which they mounted to their final result, in the delusion that like God Almighty they have built for all the ages. Neglect of the role of the individual, with resulting overemphasis on the social, may well be one of the fundamental difficulties in the way the human race handles its mind.

Attention to activities and the first person emphasizes the insight that we never get away from ourselves. Not only do I see that I cannot get away from myself, but I see that you cannot get away from yourself. The problem of how to deal with the insight that we never get away from ourselves is perhaps the most important problem before us. It is associated with, but incomparably more complicated than, the problem of the role of the observer to which quantum theory has devoted so much attention and regards as so fundamental. We consider this problem more in detail later.

Not only is each one of us as an individual not able to get away from himself, but the human race as a whole can never get away from itself. The insight that we can never get away from ourselves is an insight which the human race through its long history has been deliberately, one is tempted to say willfully, refusing to admit. But the ostensibly timeless absolutes are formulated and apprehended by us, and the vision which the mystic says is revealed by the direct intervention of God is still a vision apprehended by him. When we talk about getting away from ourselves it is we who are talking. All this is so obvious that it has only to be said, yet it seems to me to have been a major concern of most conventional philosophy and religion to sidestep the consequences of this insight, or not to admit it in the first place. A recent development in technical logic suggests that the consequences of persistent disavowal of this insight may be more disastrous than could have been suspected. The technical development was the formulation of Gödel's theorem. This theorem states that it is impossible to prove that a logical system at least as complicated as arithmetic contains no concealed contradictions by using only theorems which are derivable within the system. To prove freedom from potential contradiction it is necessary to use theorems which can be proved only by going outside the system. This theorem made a tremendous sensation, for at one stroke it stultified the attempts of some of the ablest mathematicians, such as Hilbert for example, who had long been trying to prove by mathematical principles that arithmetic or geometry contain no concealed contradictions. To prove mathematics free from potential contradiction one must use principles outside mathematics, and then to prove that these new principles do not conceal contradiction one must use new principles beyond them. The regress has no end —one has languages and meta-languages without limit.

It is exceedingly suggestive to see in Gödel's theorem an application to our present problem, the problem of discovering the consequences of not being able to get away from ourselves. It is, of course, not a question of any formal and rigorous application of the theorem, but only of something qualitative and suggestive. The essence of the situation presented by Gödel's theorem seems to be that we are here concerned with a system dealing with itself—mathematics attempting to prove something about mathematics.

Similar situations present themselves frequently in logic, as when we have the class of all classes, including itself, or contemplate the barber ordered to shave all those who do not shave themselves, including himself, or the map that must contain a map of the map. In all these situations we have systems dealing with themselves, and in all these cases we have paradox, or at best, infinite regressions, and therefore difficulty. It is tempting to generalize Gödel's theorem to read that whenever we have a system dealing with itself we may expect to encounter maladjustments and infelicities, if not downright paradox. The insight that we can never get away from ourselves obviously presents us with a situation of this sort. The brain that tries to understand is itself part of the world that it is trying to understand. It seems that the situation cannot be dealt with satisfactorily in its entirety; the best, and well-nigh all, we can do is to operate by successive approximations at different levels, isolating for treatment this or that group of phenomena which experience has shown we may hope to deal with rather satisfactorily so long as we remain within the group, but never forgetting that the concept of isolation is itself rigorously contradictory and impossible. A "level of operation" may be roughly characterized by the things we leave unanalyzed. Analysis can always be pushed further, just as we can always add one to any integer.

The insight that we can never get away from ourselves has been dramatized for me by the "demonstrations" initiated by Ames at Hanover and now carried on by Cantril and his colleagues at Princeton. In these demonstrations cunningly devised stimulations of the sense organs yield perceptions of movements in space with an inexorability that must be experienced to be appreciated, perceptions over which the subject has no control, although he knows that they are incorrect and can correspond to no possible real situation. The question obtrudes itself "What is this mold of space and time into which our perceptions so inexorably pour the world, and is it a good mold?" Evidence is accumulating that it may not always be a good mold, as when we go as far as we can into the submicroscopic world of quantum phenomena or into the world of supergalaxies. If it is not a good mold, can we invent a better? And even when we have invented it, would it not still be our mold?

The Ames-Cantril demonstrations are still the subject of controversy and many psychologists think they are of only minor significance. The insight which I acquired on witnessing the demonstrations was not a necessary or logical consequence of the experience or of the method of demonstration, and the fact that it was not probably explains why some of my psychological colleagues do not see the significance in the demonstrations that I do. Logically, it is perfectly satisfactory to say, when confronted by the physically impossible acrobatics of the crossbar in the rotating trapezoidal window, for example, that I am not perceiving things correctly in space and time. This statement, by its very form, assumes that space and time are a valid form of perception. My reaction was different and involved the logical jump of saying to myself "It may be, if my brain, which is responsible for perception, can play me such tricks in this special case, that my brain is playing me another trick in casting perceptions into the mold of space and time at all." Although this is a *non sequitur*, I think it is impossible, once one has the twist that makes one say it, to put it back where it came from and forget the vision.

Another insight is that the conceptual revolution forced by recent physical discoveries in the realm of relativity and quantum effects is not really a revolution in new realms of high velocities or the very small, but is properly a conceptual revolution on the macroscopic level of everyday life. The obvious justification of this statement is that it is still *we* who have the new concepts, and the material which goes into the formation of the concepts still comes to *us* through the agency of the same old senses. In other words, we are macroscopic creatures. It is merely that we have discovered how to make new kinds of instruments and how to do new things with them. This sort of thing is occasionally said by such exponents of conventional quantum theory as Bohr, but an appreciation of the true significance of this situation has only recently been growing upon me. The inescapable implication is that the seeds of all our recent conceptual difficulties were already with us in the way we handled the everyday common-sense world, and that if we had only made our analysis acute enough we would have been able to discover them without having to wait for the new experimental evidence. It is, of course, now too late to turn back the hands of the clock, but here is at least a stimulus to make our present analysis as penetrating as we can, to see if we cannot find some of the things that we might have said, but did not. One of the principal incentives back of this book is the conviction that there are still many new and revolutionary things to be said which have escaped us because they are so close, ubiquitous, and constant that we have not been able to see them. A conviction such as this lends a certain excitement to the attempt to make our analysis as penetrating as we can.

Another insight which we shall always try to keep in the background of any analysis is that certainty does not occur, and that sharpness and absolute rigor are unattainable. There is no adequate answer to self-doubt. This applies even to the operations of logic, traditionally supposed to be of absolute certainty. The best that we can attain is relative rigor in a limited universe of discourse and operations. It looks to me as though many philosophers and logicians do not admit this, but their ideal seems to be certainty and rigor. The recognition that these objectives can be attained only in a limited area shifts the focus of interest for me. I can, for example, no longer feel the interest in some of the analysis of symbolic logic that I formerly did. In fact, the whole enterprise of logic appears in a somewhat unconventional light, which many logicians will doubtless find heretical.

It might be thought that one's task in adjusting himself intellectually to his environment becomes easier if one gives up the ideals of absolute certainty and rigor. The exact opposite is the case—every workman knows that it is harder to work with dull tools than with sharp ones. For me, at least, the problem becomes enormously more difficult. There is in the first place the temptation to sloppy thinking—if one knows that rigor can never be attained one is tempted to do less than one's best and let a piece of analysis go that one sees could be improved if one took more time or pains with it. There are situations where a defeatist attitude is too easily adopted instead of pressing the attack to one's utmost. And there is the difficulty that one has no criterion or assurance that one has ever got to the end of the road. In the elementary geometry of my school days I could write Q. E. D. and stop thinking about it. I can now never stop thinking about any fundamental thing, but always a new idea is possible.

If the insight that one can never get away from one's self has really "got under one's skin," two diametrically opposite reactions are conceivable. Realizing the hopelessness of trying to get away from one's self, one may abandon one's self to an orgy of invention and construction of metaphysical principles and absolutes, on the principle that one might as well die for a sheep as a lamb. Or one may react by trying to get away from one's self as much as possible and to intrude one's self into any situation as little as possible. (An unsympathetic reader will have no difficulty in pointing out that there is very little meaning in the last sentence.) It was the latter ideal that inspired William of Occam long ago in his celebrated slogan that entities are not to be created beyond necessity. This appeals to me as a cardinal intellectual principle, and I will try to follow it to the utmost. It is almost frightening to observe how blatantly it is disregarded in most thinking. I do not know what logical justification can be offered for the principle. To me it seems to satisfy a deep-seated instinct for intellectual good workmanship. Perhaps one of the most compelling reasons for adopting it is that thereby one has given as few hostages to the future as possible and retained the maximum flexibility for dealing with unanticipated facts or ideas.

# J. ROBERT OPPENHEIMER

# 6: A Definition of Style

*Our final piece of testimony from science is a brief statement about* style, *by the atomic physicist J. Robert Oppenheimer. The balances and compromises suggested here are a clear consequence (in the view of this book) from a number of propositions about science and ordinary experience that have emerged from the five writers represented so far: that the sense data of our actual experience are given to us in high disorder, a fact that we disguise by the man-made rigor and neatness of language; that our neat language has lately become increasingly inadequate to express recent observations of nature; that a verbal system complete unto itself is doomed; that incongruity, flux, change are facts of life; that a necessary emphasis on the observer's own operations in science means an emphasis on the first person singular and a modest awareness of the self as limited yet powerful, humble yet the only source of wisdom there is.*

*Oppenheimer has been director of the Institute for Advanced Study at Princeton since 1947. This paragraph is from a speech he delivered in 1948 called "The Open Mind," later included in a volume of the same title.*

THE PROBLEM of doing justice to the implicit, the imponderable, and the unknown is of course not unique to politics. It is always with us in science, it is with us in the most trivial of personal affairs, and it is one of the great problems of writing and of all forms of art. The means by which it is solved is sometimes called style. It is style which complements affirmation with limitation and with humility; it is style which makes it possible to act effectively, but not absolutely; it is style which, in the domain of foreign policy, enables us to find a harmony between the pursuit of ends essential to us and the regard for the views, the sensibilities, the aspirations of those to whom the problem may appear in another light; it is style which is the deference that action pays to uncertainty; it is above all style through which power defers to reason.

# CONSEQUENCES OF THE PROBLEM:
## Testimony from Writers and Artists

JEAN-PAUL SARTRE

# 7 : Existentialism

*Now we ask the question, How does one behave in this new world the scientists have created for us—specifically, how does one express oneself? How does one, first, define what is called "the role of the individual" in an environment so drastically altered and altering? More particularly for this book, what resources of language, in painting, poetry, or plain prose, are available to such an individual who, while living in this difficult time, yet desires and needs to go on talking—and with "style"?*

*We hear first from a philosopher, who addresses himself to the first question, the role of the individual in a world where the very nature of reality has changed. That the world Jean-Paul Sartre is confronting has some relation to the world our scientists have been describing may be suggested by some close verbal similarities: Sartre's assertion below that "it is impossible for man to transcend human subjectivity" may be compared with Bridgman's on page 21 that "it is impossible to transcend the human reference point." Sartre is here defending his "doctrine of action" against his critics; by "we" and "us" (in the third sentence, for example), he simply means himself and his particular school of "existentialists." The little book from which these passages were taken was published in France in 1946 under the title* L'Existentialisme est un Humanisme, *at a time when the movement was new, fashionable, and embattled.*


MAN IS nothing else but what he makes of himself. Such is the first principle of existentialism. It is also what is called subjectivity, the name we are labeled with when charges are brought against us. But what do we mean by this, if not that man has a greater dignity than a stone or table? For we mean that man first exists, that is, that man first of all is the being who hurls himself toward a future and who is conscious of imagining himself as being in the future. Man is at the start a plan which is aware of itself, rather than a patch of moss, a piece of garbage, or a cauliflower; nothing exists prior to this plan; there is nothing in heaven; man will be what he will have planned to be. Not what he will want to be. Because by the word "will" we generally mean a conscious decision, which is subsequent to what we have already made of ourselves. I may want to belong to a political party, write a book, get married; but all that is only a manifestation of an earlier, more spontaneous choice that is called "will." But if existence really does precede essence, man is responsible for what he is. Thus, existentialism's first move is to make every man aware of what he is and to make the full responsibility of his existence rest on him. And when we say that a man is responsible for himself, we do not only mean that he is responsible for his own individuality, but that he is responsible for all men.

The word "subjectivism" has two meanings, and our opponents play on the two. Subjectivism means, on the one hand, that an individual chooses and makes himself; and, on the other, that it is impossible for man to transcend human subjectivity. The second of these is the essential meaning of existentialism. When we say that man chooses his own self, we mean that every one of us does likewise; but we also mean by that that in making this choice he also chooses all men. In fact, in creating the man that we want to be, there is not a single one of our acts which does not at the same time create an image of man as we think he ought to be. To choose to be this or that is to affirm at the same time the value of what we choose, because we can never choose evil. We always choose the good, and nothing can be good for us without being good for all.

If, on the other hand, existence precedes essence, and if we grant that we exist and fashion our image at one and the same time, the image is valid for everybody and for our whole age. Thus, our responsibility is much greater than we might have supposed, because it involves all mankind. If I am a working-man and choose to join a Christian trade union rather than be a Communist, and if by being a member I want to show that the best thing for man is resignation, that the kingdom of man is not of this world, I am not only involving my own case—I want to be resigned for everyone. As a result, my action has involved all humanity. To take a more individual matter, if I want to marry, to have children, even if this marriage depends solely on my own circumstances or passion or wish, I am involving all humanity in monogamy and not merely myself. Therefore, I am responsible for myself and for everyone else. I am creating a certain image of man of my own choosing. In choosing myself, I choose man.

This helps us understand what the actual content is of such rather grandiloquent words as anguish, forlornness, despair. As you will see, it's all quite simple.

First, what is meant by anguish? The existentialists say at once that man is anguish. What that means is this: the man who involves himself and who realizes that he is not only the person he chooses to be, but also a lawmaker who is, at the same time, choosing all mankind as well as himself, cannot help escape the feeling of his total and deep responsibility. Of course, there are many people who are not anxious; but we claim that they are hiding their anxiety, that they are fleeing from it. Certainly, many people believe that when they do something, they themselves are the only ones involved, and when someone says to them, "What if everyone acted that way?" they shrug their shoulders and answer, "Everyone doesn't act that way." But really, one should always ask himself, "What would happen if everybody looked at things that way?" There is no escaping this disturbing thought except by a kind of double-dealing. A man who lies and makes excuses for himself by saying "not everybody does that," is someone with an uneasy conscience, because the act of lying implies that a universal value is conferred upon the lie.

Anguish is evident even when it conceals itself. This is the anguish that Kierkegaard called the anguish of Abraham. You know the story: an angel has ordered Abraham to sacrifice his son; if it really were an angel who has come and said, "You are Abraham, you shall sacrifice your son," everything would be all right. But everyone might first wonder, "Is it really an angel, and am I really Abraham? What proof do I have?"

There was a madwoman who had hallucinations; someone used to speak to her on the telephone and give her orders. Her doctor asked her, "Who is it who talks to you?" She answered, "He says it's God." What proof did she really have that it was God? If an angel comes to me, what proof is there that it's an angel? And if I hear voices, what proof is there that they come from heaven and not from hell, or from the subconscious, or a pathological condition? What proves that they are addressed to me? What proof is there that I have been appointed to impose my choice and my conception of man on humanity? I'll never find any proof or sign to convince me of that. If a voice addresses me, it is always for me to decide that this is the angel's voice; if I consider that such an act is a good one, it is I who will choose to say that it is good rather than bad.

Now, I'm not being singled out as an Abraham, and yet at every moment I'm obliged to perform exemplary acts. For every man, everything happens as if all mankind had its eyes fixed on him and were guiding itself by what he does. And every man ought to say to himself, "Am I really the kind of man who has the right to act in such a way that humanity might guide itself by my actions?" And if he does not say that to himself, he is masking his anguish.

There is no question here of the kind of anguish which would lead to quietism, to inaction. It is a matter of a simple sort of anguish that anybody who has had responsibilities is familiar with. For example, when a military officer takes the responsibility for an attack and sends a certain number of men to death, he chooses to do so, and in the main he alone makes the choice. Doubtless, orders come from above, but they are too broad; he interprets them, and on this interpretation depend the lives of ten or fourteen or twenty men. In making a decision he cannot help having a certain anguish. All leaders know this anguish. That doesn't keep them from acting; on the contrary, it is the very condition of their action. For it implies that they envisage a number of possibilities, and when they choose one, they realize that it has value only because it is chosen. We shall see that this kind of anguish, which is the kind that existentialism describes, is explained, in addition, by a direct responsibility to the other men whom it involves. It is not a curtain separating us from action, but is part of action itself.

When we speak of forlornness, a term Heidegger was fond of, we mean only that God does not exist and that we have to face all the consequences of this. The existentialist is strongly opposed to a certain kind of secular ethics which would like to abolish God with the least possible expense. About 1880, some French teachers tried to set up a secular ethics which went something like this: God is a useless and costly hypothesis; we are discarding it; but, meanwhile, in order for there to be an ethics, a society, a civilization, it is essential that certain values be taken seriously and that they be considered as having an *a priori* existence. It must be obligatory, *a priori*, to be honest, not to lie, not to beat your wife, to have children, etc., etc. So we're going to try a little device which will make it possible to show that values exist all the same, inscribed in a heaven of ideas, though otherwise God does not exist. In other words—and this, I believe, is the tendency of everything called reformism in France—nothing will be changed if God does not exist. We shall find ourselves with the same norms of honesty, progress, and humanism, and we shall have made of God an outdated hypothesis which will peacefully die off by itself.

The existentialist, on the contrary, thinks it very distressing that God does not exist, because all possibility of finding values in a heaven of ideas disappears along with Him; there can no longer be an *a priori* Good, since there is no infinite and perfect consciousness to think it. Nowhere is it written that the Good exists, that we must be honest, that we must not lie; because the fact is we are on a plane where there are only men. Dostoievsky said, "If God didn't exist, everything would be possible." That is the very starting point of existentialism. Indeed, everything is permissible if God does not exist, and as a result man is forlorn, because neither within him nor without does he find anything to cling to. He can't start making excuses for himself.

If existence really does precede essence, there is no explaining things away by reference to a fixed and given human nature. In other words, there is no determinism, man is free, man is freedom. On the other hand, if God does not exist, we find no values or commands to turn to which legitimize our conduct. So, in the bright realm of values, we have no excuse behind us, nor justification before us. We are alone, with no excuses.

That is the idea I shall try to convey when I say that man is condemned to be free. Condemned, because he did not create himself, yet, in other respects is free; because, once thrown into the world, he is responsible for everything he does. The existentialist does not believe in the power of passion. He will never agree that a sweeping passion is a ravaging torrent which fatally leads a man to certain acts and is therefore an excuse. He thinks that man is responsible for his passion.

The existentialist does not think that man is going to help himself by finding in the world some omen by which to orient himself. Because he thinks that man will interpret the omen to suit himself. Therefore, he thinks that man, with no support and no aid, is condemned every moment to invent man. Ponge, in a very fine article, has said, "Man is the future of man." That's exactly it. But if it is taken to mean that this future is recorded in heaven, that God sees it, then it is false, because it would really no longer be a future. If it is taken to mean that, whatever a man may be, there is a future to be forged, a virgin future before him, then this remark is sound. But then we are forlorn.

To give you an example which will enable you to understand forlornness better, I shall cite the case of one of my students who came to see me under the following circumstances: his father was on bad terms with his mother, and, moreover, was inclined to be a collaborationist; his older brother had been killed in the German offensive of 1940, and the young man, with somewhat immature but generous feelings, wanted to avenge him. His mother lived alone with him, very much upset by the half-treason of her husband and the death of her older son; the boy was her only consolation.

The boy was faced with the choice of leaving for England and joining the Free French forces—that is, leaving his mother behind—or remaining with his mother and helping her to carry on. He was fully aware that the woman lived only for him and that his going off—and perhaps his death— would plunge her into despair. He was also aware that every act that he did for his mother's sake was a sure thing, in the sense that it was helping her to carry on, whereas every effort he made toward going off and fighting was an uncertain move which might run aground and prove completely useless; for example, on his way to England he might, while passing through Spain, be detained indefinitely in a Spanish camp; he might reach England or Algiers and be stuck in an office at a desk job. As a result, he was faced with two very different kinds of action: one, concrete, immediate, but concerning only one individual; the other concerned an incomparably vaster group, a national collectivity, but for that very reason was dubious, and might be interrupted en route. And, at the same time, he was wavering between two kinds of ethics. On the one hand, an ethics of sympathy, of personal devotion; on the other, a broader ethics, but one whose efficacy was more dubious. He had to choose between the two.

Who could help him choose? Christian doctrine? No. Christian doctrine says, "Be charitable, love your neighbor, take the more rugged path, etc., etc." But which is the more rugged path? Whom should he love as a brother? The fighting man or his mother? Which does the greater good, the vague act of fighting in a group, or the concrete one of helping a particular human being to go on living? Who can decide *a priori*? Nobody. No book of ethics can tell him. The Kantian ethics says, "Never treat any person as a means, but as an end." Very well, if I stay with my mother, I'll treat her as an end and not as a means; but by virtue of this very fact, I'm running the risk of treating the people around me who are fighting, as means; and, conversely, if I go to join those who are fighting, I'll be treating them as an end, and, by doing that, I run the risk of treating my mother as a means.

If values are vague, and if they are always too broad for the concrete and specific case that we are considering, the only thing left for us is to trust our instincts. That's what this young man tried to do; and when I saw him, he said, "In the end, feeling is what counts. I ought to choose whichever pushes me in one direction. If I feel that I love my mother enough to sacrifice everything else for her—my desire for vengeance, for action, for adventure—then I'll stay with her. If, on the contrary, I feel that my love for my mother isn't enough, I'll leave."

But how is the value of a feeling determined? What gives his feeling for his mother value? Precisely the fact that he remained with her. I may say that I like so-and-so well enough to sacrifice a certain amount of money for him, but I may say so only if I've done it. I may say "I love my mother well enough to remain with her" if I have remained with her. The only way to determine the value of this affection is, precisely, to perform an act which confirms and defines it. But, since I require this affection to justify my act, I find myself caught in a vicious circle.

On the other hand, Gide has well said that a mock feeling and a true feeling are almost indistinguishable; to decide that I love my mother and will remain with her, or to remain with her by putting on an act, amount somewhat to the same thing. In other words, the feeling is formed by the acts one performs; so, I cannot refer to it in order to act upon it. Which means that I can neither seek within myself the true condition which will impel me to act, nor apply to a system of ethics for concepts which will permit me to act. You will say, "At least, he did go to a teacher for advice." But if you seek advice from a priest, for example, you have chosen this priest; you already knew, more or less, just about what advice he was going to give you. In other words, choosing your adviser is involving yourself. The proof of this is that if you are a Christian, you will say, "Consult a priest." But some priests are collaborating, some are just marking time, some are resisting. Which to choose? If the young man chooses a priest who is resisting or collaborating, he has already decided on the kind of advice he's going to get. Therefore, in coming to see me he knew the answer I was going to give him, and I had only one answer to give: "You're free, choose, that is, invent." No general ethics can show you what is to be done; there are no omens in the world. The Catholics will reply, "But there are." Granted—but, in any case, I myself choose the meaning they have.

When I was a prisoner, I knew a rather remarkable young

man who was a Jesuit. He had entered the Jesuit order in the following way: he had had a number of very bad breaks; in childhood, his father died, leaving him in poverty, and he was a scholarship student at a religious institution where he was constantly made to feel that he was being kept out of charity; then, he failed to get any of the honors and distinctions that children like; later on, at about eighteen, he bungled a love affair; finally, at twenty-two, he failed in military training, a childish enough matter, but it was the last straw.

This young fellow might well have felt that he had botched everything. It was a sign of something, but of what? He might have taken refuge in bitterness or despair. But he very wisely looked upon all this as a sign that he was not made for secular triumphs, and that only the triumphs of religion, holiness, and faith were open to him. He saw the hand of God in all this, and so he entered the order. Who can help seeing that he alone decided what the sign meant?

Some other interpretation might have been drawn from this series of setbacks; for example, that he might have done better to turn carpenter or revolutionist. Therefore, he is fully responsible for the interpretation. Forlornness implies that we ourselves choose our being. Forlornness and anguish go together.

As for despair, the term has a very simple meaning. It means that we shall confine ourselves to reckoning only with what depends upon our will, or on the ensemble of probabilities which make our action possible. When we want something, we always have to reckon with probabilities. I may be counting on the arrival of a friend. The friend is coming by rail or streetcar; this supposes that the train will arrive on schedule, or that the streetcar will not jump the track. I am left in the realm of possibility; but possibilities are to be reckoned with only to the point where my action comports with the ensemble of these possibilities, and no further. The moment the possibilities I am considering are not rigorously involved by my action, I ought to disengage myself from them, because no God, no scheme, can adapt the world and its possibilities to my will. When Descartes said, "Conquer yourself rather than the world," he meant essentially the same thing.

The Marxists to whom I have spoken reply, "You can rely on the support of others in your action, which obviously has certain limits because you're not going to live forever. That means: rely on both what others are doing elsewhere to help you, in China, in Russia, and what they will do later on, after your death, to carry on the action and lead it to its fulfillment, which will be the revolution. You even *have* to rely upon that, otherwise you're immoral." I reply at once that I will always rely on fellow-fighters insofar as these comrades are involved with me in a common struggle, in the unity of a party or a group in which I can more or less make my weight felt; that is, one whose ranks I am in as a fighter and whose movements I am aware of at every moment. In such a situation, relying on the unity and will of the party is exactly like counting on the fact that the train will arrive on time or that the car won't jump the track. But, given that man is free and that there is no human nature for me to depend on, I cannot count on men whom I do not know by relying on human goodness or man's concern for the good of society. I don't know what will become of the Russian revolution; I may make an example of it to the extent that at the present time it is apparent that the proletariat plays a part in Russia that it plays in no other nation. But I can't swear that this will inevitably lead to a triumph of the proletariat. I've got to limit myself to what I see.

Given that men are free and that tomorrow they will freely decide what man will be, I cannot be sure that, after my death, fellow-fighters will carry on my work to bring it to its maximum perfection. Tomorrow, after my death, some men may decide to set up Fascism, and the others may be cowardly and muddled enough to let them do it. Fascism will then be the human reality, so much the worse for us.

Actually, things will be as man will have decided they are

to be. Does that mean that I should abandon myself to quietism? No. First, I should involve myself; then, act on the old saw, "Nothing ventured, nothing gained." Nor does it mean that I shouldn't belong to a party, but rather that I shall have no illusions and shall do what I can. For example, suppose I ask myself, "Will socialization, as such, ever come about?" I know nothing about it. All I know is that I'm going to do everything in my power to bring it about. Beyond that, I can't count on anything. Quietism is the attitude of people who say, "Let others do what I can't do." The doctrine I am presenting is the very opposite of quietism, since it declares, "There is no reality except in action." Moreover, it goes further, since it adds, "Man is nothing else than his plan; he exists only to the extent that he fulfills himself; he is therefore nothing else than the ensemble of his acts, nothing else than his life."

According to this, we can understand why our doctrine horrifies certain people. Because often the only way they can bear their wretchedness is to think, "Circumstances have been against me. What I've been and done doesn't show my true worth. To be sure, I've had no great love, no great friendship, but that's because I haven't met a man or woman who was worthy. The books I've written haven't been very good because I haven't had the proper leisure. I haven't had children to devote myself to because I didn't find a man with whom I could have spent my life. So there remains within me, unused and quite viable, a host of propensities, inclinations, possibilities, that one wouldn't guess from the mere series of things I've done."

Now, for the existentialist there is really no love other than one which manifests itself in a person's being in love. There is no genius other than one which is expressed in works of art; the genius of Proust is the sum of Proust's works; the genius of Racine is his series of tragedies. Outside of that, there is nothing. Why say that Racine could have written another tragedy, when he didn't write it? A man is involved in life, leaves his impress on it, and outside of that there is nothing. To be sure, this may seem a harsh thought to someone whose life hasn't been a success. But, on the other hand, it prompts people to understand that reality alone is what counts, that dreams, expectations, and hopes warrant no more than to define a man as a disappointed dream, as miscarried hopes, as vain expectations. In other words, to define him negatively and not positively. However, when we say, "You are nothing else than your life," that does not imply that the artist will be judged solely on the basis of his works of art; a thousand other things will contribute toward summing him up. What we mean is that a man is nothing else than a series of undertakings, that he is the sum, the organization, the ensemble of the relationships which make up these undertakings.

When all is said and done, what we are accused of, at bottom, is not our pessimism, but an optimistic toughness. If people throw up to us our works of fiction in which we write about people who are soft, weak, cowardly, and sometimes even downright bad, it's not because these people are soft, weak, cowardly, or bad; because if we were to say, as Zola did, that they are that way because of heredity, the workings of environment, society, because of biological or psychological determinism, people would be reassured. They would say, "Well, that's what we're like, no one can do anything about it." But when the existentialist writes about a coward, he says that this coward is responsible for his cowardice. He's not like that because he has a cowardly heart or lung or brain; he's not like that on account of his physiological make-up; but he's like that because he has made himself a coward by his acts. There's no such thing as a cowardly constitution; there are nervous constitutions; there is poor blood, as the common people say, or strong constitutions. But the man whose blood is poor is not a coward on that account, for what makes cowardice is the act of renouncing or yielding. A constitution is not an act; the coward is defined on the basis of the acts he performs. People feel, in a vague sort of way, that this coward

we're talking about is guilty of being a coward, and the
thought frightens them. What people would like is that a
coward or a hero be born that way. . . .

From these few reflections it is evident that nothing is more
unjust than the objections that have been raised against us.
Existentialism is nothing else than an attempt to draw all the
consequences of a coherent atheistic position. It isn't trying to
plunge man into despair at all. But if one calls every attitude
of unbelief despair, like the Christians, then the word is not
being used in its original sense. Existentialism isn't so atheistic
that it wears itself out showing that God doesn't exist. Rather,
it declares that even if God did exist, that would change nothing. There you've got our point of view. Not that we believe
that God exists, but we think that the problem of His existence is not the issue. In this sense existentialism is optimistic, a
doctrine of action, and it is plain dishonesty for Christians to
make no distinction between their own despair and ours and
then to call us despairing.

# WILLIAM BARRETT

# 8: Testimony of Modern Art

*This passage is by a commentator on Sartre and Existentialism, and it attempts to relate the flatness and lack of realism in modern painting, particularly Cubism, to the kind of world that Sartre has described. The presentation of experience as a chaos of disconnected details, without order or climax (guitars, oranges, spools of thread), offers obvious analogies to the statements about "actual experience" by James and Whitehead with which this collection began. Furthermore, Barrett's comment, with respect to artists, that "the final intelligibility of the world is no longer accepted," suggests an important likeness between the painter's situation and that of the modern scientist as described by Conant and Bridgman. The break with tradition would appear to be just as drastic and fundamental in the painter's activity as in the scientist's or philosopher's.*

*Mr. Barrett, formerly editor of* Partisan Review, *is professor of philosophy at New York University.*

A GREAT formal style in painting has never been created that did not draw upon the depths of the human spirit, and that did not, in its newness, express a fresh mutation of the human spirit. Cubism achieved a radical flattening of space by insisting on the two-dimensional fact of the canvas. This flattening out of space would seem not to be a negligible fact historically if we reflect that when, once before in history, such a development occurred but in the opposite direction— when the flatness of the Gothic or primitive painters passed over into the solidity, perspective, and three-dimensional style of early Renaissance painting—it was a mark that man was turning outward, into space, after the long period of introspection of the Middle Ages. Western man moved out into space in his painting, in the fourteenth century, before he set forth into actual physical space in the age of exploration that was to follow. Thus painting was prophetic of the new turn of the human spirit which was eventually to find expression in the conquest of the whole globe. Have we the right, then, to suggest that the flattening of painting in our own century portends a turning inward of the human spirit, or at any rate a turning away from that outer world of space which has hitherto been the ultimate arena of Western man's extroversion? With Cubism begins that process of detachment from the object which has become the hallmark of modern art. Even though Cubism is a classical and formal style, the artist nevertheless asserts his own subjectivity by the freedom with which he cuts up and dislocates objects—bottles, pitchers, guitars—as it pleases him for the sake of the picture, which is now no longer held up to us as a representation of those objects but as a visual image with its own independent value alongside that of nature. The subjectivity that is generally present in modern art is a psychological compensation for, sometimes a violent revolt against, the gigantic externalization of life within modern society. The world pictured by the modern artist is, like the world meditated upon by the existential philosopher, a world where man is a stranger.

When mankind no longer lives spontaneously turned toward God or the supersensible world—when, to echo the words of Yeats, the ladder is gone by which we would climb to a higher reality—the artist too must stand face to face with a flat and inexplicable world. This shows itself even in the formal structures of modern art. Where the movement of the spirit is no longer vertical but only horizontal, the climactic elements in art are in general leveled out, flattened. The flattening of pictorial space that is achieved in Cubism is not an isolated fact, true only of painting, but is paralleled by similar changes in literary techniques. There is a general process of flattening, three chief aspects of which may be noted:

(1) *The flattening out of all planes* upon the plane of the picture. Near and far are pushed together. So in certain works of modern literature time, instead of space, is flattened out upon one plane. Past and present are represented as occurring simultaneously, upon a single plane of time. James Joyce's *Ulysses*, T. S. Eliot's *The Waste Land*, and Ezra Pound's *Cantos* are examples; and perhaps the most powerful use of the device was made by Faulkner in his early novel *The Sound and the Fury*.

(2) More important perhaps is *the flattening out of climaxes*, which occurs both in painting and literature. In traditional Western painting there is a central subject, located at or near the center of the picture, and the surrounding space in the picture is subordinate to this. In a portrait the figure is placed near the center, and the background becomes secondary to it, something to be blended as harmoniously as possible with the figure. Cubism abolished this idea of the pictorial climax: the whole space of the picture became of equal importance. Negative spaces (in which there are no objects) are as important as positive spaces (the contours of physical objects). If a human figure is treated, it may be broken up and distributed over various parts of the canvas. Formally speaking, the spirit of this art is anticlimactic.

When we turn to observe this same deflation or flattening of climaxes in literature, the broader human and philosophic questions involved become much clearer. The classical tradition in literature, deriving from Aristotle's *Poetics*, tells us that a drama (and consequently any other literary work) must have a beginning, middle, and end. The action begins at a certain point, rises toward a climax, and then falls to a dénouement. One can diagram a classical plot of this kind by means of a triangle whose apex represents the climax with which everything in the play has some logical and necessary connection. The author subordinates himself to the requirements of logic, necessity, probability. His structure must be an intelligible whole in which each part develops logically out of what went before. If our existence itself is never quite like this, no matter; art is a selection from life, and the poet is required to be selective. However, it is important to note that this canon of intelligible literary structure—beginning, middle, and end, with a well-defined climax—arose in a culture in which the universe too was believed to be an ordered structure, a rational and intelligible whole.

What happens if we try to apply this classical Aristotelian canon to a modern work like Joyce's *Ulysses*, 734 pages of power and dullness, beauty and sordidness, comedy and pathos, where the movement is always horizontal, never ascending toward any crisis, and where we detect not the shadow of anything like a climax, in the traditional sense of that term? If Joyce's had been a disordered mind, we could dismiss all this as a sprawling chaos; but he was in fact an artist in superb control of his material, so that the disorder has to be attributed to his material, to life itself. It is, in fact, the banal gritty thing that we live that Joyce gives us, in comparison with which most other fiction is indeed fiction. This world is dense, opaque, unintelligible; that is the datum from which the modern artist always starts. The formal dictates of the well-made play or the well-made novel, which were the logical outcome of thoroughly rational preconceptions about reality, we can no longer hold to when we become attentive "to the things themselves," to the facts, to existence in the mode in which we do exist. If our epoch still held to the idea, as Western man once did, that the whole of reality is a system in which each detail providentially and rationally is subordinated to others and ultimately to the whole itself, we could demand of the artist that his form imitate this idea of reality, and give us coherence, logic, and the picture of a world with no loose ends. But to make such a demand nowadays is worse than an impertinence: it is a travesty upon the historical being of the artist. . . .

That the Western artist now finds his own inherited classical form unconvincing and indeed almost intolerable is because of a profound change in his total attitude toward the world—a change that is no less true even when the artist himself has not been able to bring it to conceptual expression. The final intelligibility of the world is no longer accepted. Our existence, as we know it, is no longer transparent and understandable by reason, bound together into a tight, coherent structure. The world that we are shown in the work of the modern painters and writers is opaque and dense. Their vision is not inspired primarily by intellectual premises; it is a spontaneous revelation of the kind of which perhaps only art is capable: it shows us where we stand, whether or not we choose to understand it. If we really open ourselves to the experience of two works of art as widely separated in time as Dante's *Divine Comedy* and Faulkner's *The Sound and the Fury*, the distance that Western man has traveled in the intervening centuries is revealed to us more clearly than through any number of abstract arguments. And the road that has been traveled is irreversible.

(3) The last and most important aspect of what we have called the process of flattening in modern art is *the flattening out of values*. To understand this one can begin at the simplest level in painting, where it means merely that large and small objects are treated as of equal value. Cézanne paints apples with the same passionate concentration as he paints mountains, and each apple is as monumental as a mountain. Indeed, in some of Cézanne's still lifes, if one covers up all of the picture except a certain patch of folded tablecloth, one might very well be looking at the planes and peaks of his Mont St. Victoire. For Cézanne the painting dictates its own

values: little and big, high and low, sublime and ordinary outside the painting are of equal importance if in a given painting they play the same plastic role.

Now all this is quite contrary to the great tradition of Western art, which distinguishes sharply between the sublime and the banal and requires that the highest art treat the most sublime subjects. The mind of the West has always been hierarchical: the cosmos has been understood as a great chain of Being, from highest to lowest, which has at the same time operated as a scale of values, from lowest to highest. Painters were expected to portray the sublime scenes from the Gospel, great battles, or noble personages. The beginning of genre painting in the seventeenth century was the first step toward what we now think of as modern painting, but it was not until the present century that the reversal of Western values was really accomplished. By now, the hierarchical scheme has been abolished altogether. Following Cézanne, the Cubists took as subjects for their most monumental paintings ordinary objects like tables, bottles, glasses, guitars. Now the painter dispenses with objects altogether: the colored shape on his canvas is itself an absolute reality, perhaps more so than the imaginary scene, the great battle, which in a traditional canvas it might serve to depict. Thus we arrive at last at *l'art brut* (raw, crude, or brute art), which seeks to abolish not only the ironclad distinction between the sublime and the banal but that between the beautiful and the ugly as well. . . .

Such ideas seem scandalous to the Western traditionalist; they undermine the time-honored canon of beauty, countenance the most disorderly elements in existence, and strike against art itself. Yet they are ideas that might be easily understood by an Oriental. For the Oriental, opposites have never been put into separate water-tight compartments as with the Westerner: as it is above, so it is below, in the East; the small is equal to the great, for amid the endless expanse of countless universes, each individual universe is as but a grain of sand on the shores of the Ganges, and a grain of sand is the equal of a universe. The lotus blooms in the mud; and generally the Oriental is as willing, in his indifference, to accept the ugly dross of existence as he is its beauty, where the Westerner might very well gag at the taste. We are not concerned here with the question of whether the West is now moving toward forms of thinking and feeling that are closer to what were once those of the East. What is of concern to the philosopher is the fact that here, in art, we find so many signs of a break with the Western tradition, or at least with what had been thought to be *the* Western tradition; the philosopher must occupy himself with this break if he is to recast the meaning of this tradition.

The deflation, or flattening out, of values in Western art does not necessarily indicate an ethical nihilism. Quite the contrary; in opening our eyes to the rejected elements of existence, art may lead us to a more complete and less artificial celebration of the world. In literature, again, the crucial example is Joyce's *Ulysses*. It was not a literary critic but a psychologist, C. G. Jung, who perceived that this book was non-Western in spirit; he sees it as Oriental to such an extent that he recommends it as a much-needed bible to the white-skinned races. For *Ulysses* breaks with the whole tradition of Western sensibility and Western aesthetics in showing each small object of Bloom's day—even the objects in his pocket, like a cake of soap—as capable at certain moments of taking on a transcendental importance—or in being, at any rate, equal in value to those objects to which men usually attribute transcendental importance. Each grain of sand, Joyce seems to be saying (as the Oriental says), reflects the whole universe —and the Irish writer was not in the least a mystic; he simply takes experience as it comes, in the course of the single day he depicts in the novel. Any such break with tradition, where a serious reversal of values is involved, is of course dangerous, for the artist runs the risk of losing the safeguards that the experience of the past has erected for him. A good deal of modern art has clearly succumbed to this danger, and the result is disorder in the art and the artist; but the danger is the price that must be paid for any step forward by the human spirit. . . .

Through modern art our time reveals itself to itself, or at least to those persons who are willing to look at their own age dispassionately and without the blindness of preconceptions, in the looking glass of its art. In our epoch existential philosophy has appeared as an intellectual expression of the time, and this philosophy exhibits numerous points of contact with modern art. The more closely we examine the two together, the stronger becomes the impression that existential philosophy is the authentic intellectual expression of our time, as modern art is the expression of the time in terms of image and intuition.

Not only do the two treat similar themes, but both start off from the sense of crisis and of a break in the Western tradition. Modern art has discarded the traditional assumptions of rational form. The modern artist sees man not as the rational animal, in the sense handed down to the West by the Greeks, but as something else. Reality, too, reveals itself to the artist not as the Great Chain of Being, which the tradition of Western rationalism had declared intelligible down to its smallest link and in its totality, but as much more refractory: as opaque, dense, concrete, and in the end inexplicable. At the limits of reason one comes face to face with the meaningless; and the artist today shows us the absurd, the inexplicable, the meaningless in our daily life.

This break with the Western tradition imbues both philosophy and art with the sense that everything is questionable, problematic. Our time, said Max Scheler, is the first in which man has become thoroughly and completely problematic to himself. Hence the themes that obsess both modern art and existential philosophy are the alienation and strangeness of man in his world; the contradictoriness, feebleness, and contingency of human existence; the central and overwhelming reality of time for man who has lost his anchorage in the eternal.

The testimony art brings to these themes is all the more convincing in that it is spontaneous; it does not spring from ideas or from any intellectual program. That modern art which is most successful and powerful moves us because we see in it the artist subordinate (as must always be the case in art) to his vision. And since we recognize that man's being is historical through and through, we must take this vision of modern art as a sign that the image of man which has been at the center of our tradition till now must be re-evaluated and recast.

There is a painful irony in the new image of man that is emerging, however fragmentarily, from the art of our time. An observer from another planet might well be struck by the disparity between the enormous power which our age has concentrated in its external life and the inner poverty which our art seeks to expose to view. This is, after all, the age that has discovered and harnessed atomic energy, that has made airplanes that fly faster than the sun, and that will, in a few years (perhaps in a few months), have atomic-powered planes which can fly through outer space and not need to return to mother earth for weeks. What cannot man do! He has greater power now than Prometheus or Icarus or any of those daring mythical heroes who were later to succumb to the disaster of pride. But if an observer from Mars were to turn his attention from these external appurtenances of power to the shape of man as revealed in our novels, plays, painting, and sculpture, he would find there a creature full of holes and gaps, faceless, riddled with doubts and negations, starkly finite.

However disconcerting this violent contrast between power and impoverishment, there is something a little consoling in it for anyone who is intimidated by excessive material power, as there is in learning that a dictator is a drunkard or marked by some other ordinary failing which makes him seem a trifle more human. If we are to redeem any part of our world from the brute march of power, we may have to begin as modern art does by exalting some of the humble and dirty little corners of existence. On another level, however, this violent contrast is frightening, for it represents a dangerous lagging of man behind his own works; and in this lag lies the terror of the atomic bomb which hangs over us like impending night. Here surely the ordinary man begins to catch a fleeting glimpse of that Nothingness which both artist and philosopher have begun in our time to take seriously. The bomb reveals the dreadful and total contingency of human existence. Existentialism is the philosophy of the atomic age.

GERTRUDE STEIN

# 9: Parts of Speech and Punctuation

*If there is any truth to the statements we have been encoun-
tering so far in this book, then the world that the "thinking
man" must face up to is a world loaded with complexities and
ambiguities, with admissions of a final unintelligibility of life,
with enormous responsibility of the individual person in a god-
less universe. To many readers, perhaps, all this is obvious
enough. What does it imply about man's actual day-to-day
use of language? For example, what changes have occurred in
the way people talk about grammar, punctuation, parts of
speech, that sort of thing? Actually people who are supposed to
think about such things—English teachers in particular—have
in the past half-century matured and developed a good deal
less than scientists, philosophers, or painters. The interested
reader, however, may wish to consult recent works on "structural linguistics," a theory of grammar more in accord with the
facts of changing English usage which may eventually bring
the teaching of elementary structure more up to date.*

*Meanwhile, for a spectacularly fresh look at grammar from
a distinctively twentieth-century point of view, we will look
elsewhere, and thirty years back. Gertrude Stein, in the passage
that follows, has things to say about punctuation and parts of
speech that only a person living very much in "our time"
could say. (I do not mean that modern structural linguists
would agree with all of them.) She says them, moreover, in her*

79

*characteristic manner suggesting by the very rhythm and order of the words that the old ways of expression are dead. Miss Stein's comfort in a world of flux and change is evident in what she says about punctuation and parts of speech, however remote her remarks may seem to a reader who wants to know where he "ought" to place a comma. Her preference for moving verbs, especially participles, over the more static nouns and adjectives, speaks for itself. Her antagonism to commas—almost any commas—is really a defense of ambiguity, a protection against being taken too simply. Her echoing of the speech patterns and vocabulary of ordinary conversation, and her wit, are protections against being taken too solemnly. Two things about Gertrude Stein's life are worth adding for our purposes here: that she received an excellent scientific education in her youth (Whitehead later became one of her idols), and that she was among the very earliest to appreciate and buy Cubist paintings.*

*The passage here is taken from a lecture called "Poetry and Grammar," one of several lectures Miss Stein delivered to delighted or amazed audiences during a triumphant tour of her native America in the thirties.*

ONE OF the things that is a very interesting thing to know is how you are feeling inside you to the words that are coming out to be outside of you.

Do you always have the same kind of feeling in relation to the sounds as the words come out of you or do you not. All this has so much to do with grammar and with poetry and with prose.

Words have to do everything in poetry and prose and some writers write more in articles and prepositions and some say you should write in nouns, and of course one has to think of everything.

A noun is a name of anything, why after a thing is named write about it. A name is adequate or it is not. If it is adequate then why go on calling it, if it is not then calling it by its name does no good.

People if you like to believe it can be made by their names. Call anybody Paul and they get to be a Paul call anybody Alice and they get to be an Alice perhaps yes perhaps no, there is something in that, but generally speaking, things once they are named the name does not go on doing anything to them and so why write in nouns. Nouns are the name of anything and just naming names is alright when you want to call a roll but is it any good for anything else. To be sure in many places in Europe as in America they do like to call rolls.

As I say a noun is a name of a thing, and therefore slowly if you feel what is inside that thing you do not call it by the name by which it is known. Everybody knows that by the way they do when they are in love and a writer should always have that intensity of emotion about whatever is the object about which he writes. And therefore and I say it again more and more one does not use nouns.

Now what other things are there beside nouns, there are a lot of other things beside nouns.

When you are at school and learn grammar grammar is very exciting. I really do not know that anything has ever been more exciting than diagraming sentences. I suppose other things may be more exciting to others when they are at school but to me undoubtedly when I was at school the really completely exciting thing was diagraming sentences and that has been to me ever since the one thing that has been completely exciting and completely completing. I like the feeling the everlasting feeling of sentences as they diagram themselves.

In that way one is completely possessing something and incidentally one's self. Now in that diagraming of the sentences of course there are articles and prepositions and as I say there are nouns but nouns as I say even by definition are completely not interesting, the same thing is true of adjectives. Adjectives are not really and truly interesting. In a way anybody can know always has known that, because after all adjectives effect nouns and as nouns are not really interesting the thing that effects a not too interesting thing is of necessity not interesting. In a way as I say anybody knows that because of course the first thing that anybody takes out of anybody's writing are the adjectives. You see of yourself how true it is that which I have just said.

Beside the nouns and the adjectives there are verbs and adverbs. Verbs and adverbs are more interesting. In the first place they have one very nice quality and that is that they can be so mistaken. It is wonderful the number of mistakes a verb can make and that is equally true of its adverb. Nouns and adjectives never can make mistakes can never be mistaken but verbs can be so endlessly, both as to what they do and how they agree or disagree with whatever they do. The same is true of adverbs.

In that way any one can see that verbs and adverbs are more interesting than nouns and adjectives.

Beside being able to be mistaken and to make mistakes verbs can change to look like themselves or to look like something else, they are, so to speak on the move and adverbs move with them and each of them find themselves not at all annoying but very often very much mistaken. That is the reason any one can like what verbs can do. Then comes the thing that can of all things be most mistaken and they are prepositions. Prepositions can live one long life being really being nothing but absolutely nothing but mistaken and that makes them irritating if you feel that way about mistakes but certainly something that you can be continuously using and everlastingly enjoying. I like prepositions the best of all, and pretty soon we will go more completely into that.

Then there are articles. Articles are interesting just as nouns and adjectives are not. And why are they interesting just as nouns and adjectives are not. They are interesting because they do what a noun might do if a noun was not so unfortunately so completely unfortunately the name of something. Articles please, a and an and the please as the name that follows cannot please. They the names that is the nouns cannot please, because after all you know well after all that is what Shakespeare meant when he talked about a rose by any other name.

I hope now no one can have any illusion about a noun or about the adjective that goes with the noun.

But an article an article remains as a delicate and a varied something and any one who wants to write with articles and knows how to use them will always have the pleasure that using something that is varied and alive can give. That is what articles are.

Beside that there are conjunctions, and a conjunction is not varied but it has a force that need not make any one feel that they are dull. Conjunctions have made themselves live by their work. They work and as they work they live and even when they do not work and in these days they do not always live by work still nevertheless they do live.

So you see why I like to write with prepositions and conjunctions and articles and verbs and adverbs but not with nouns and adjectives. If you read my writing you will you do see what I mean.

Of course then there are pronouns. Pronouns are not as bad as nouns because in the first place practically they cannot have adjectives go with them. That already makes them better than nouns.

Then beside not being able to have adjectives go with them, they of course are not really the name of anything. They represent some one but they are not its or his name. In not being his or its or her name they already have a greater possibility of being something than if they were as a noun is the name of anything. Now actual given names of people are more lively than nouns which are the name of anything and I suppose that this is because after all the name is only given to that person when they are born, there is at least the element of choice even the element of change and anybody can be pretty well able to do what they like, they may be born Walter and become Hub, in such a way they are not like a noun. A noun has been the name of something for such a very long time.

That is the reason that slang exists it is to change the nouns which have been names for so long. I say again. Verbs and adverbs and articles and conjunctions and prepositions are lively because they all do something and as long as anything does something it keeps alive.

One might have in one's list added interjections but really interjections have nothing to do with anything not even with themselves. There so much for that. And now to go into the question of punctuation.

There are some punctuations that are interesting and there are some punctuations that are not. Let us begin with the punctuations that are not. Of these the one but the first and the most the completely most uninteresting is the question mark. The question mark is alright when it is all alone when it is used as a brand on cattle or when it could be used in decoration but connected with writing it is completely entirely completely uninteresting. It is evident that if you ask a question you ask a question but anybody who can read at all knows when a question is a question as it is written in writing. Therefore I ask you therefore wherefore should one use it the question mark. Beside it does not in its form go with ordinary printing and so it pleases neither the eye nor the ear and it is therefore like a noun, just an unnecessary name of something. A question is a question, anybody can know that a question is a question and so why add to it the question mark when it is already there when the question is already there in the writing. Therefore I never could bring myself to use a question mark, I always found it positively revolting, and now very few do use it. Exclamation marks have the same difficulty and also quotation marks, they are unnecessary, they are ugly, they spoil the line of the writing or the printing and anyway what is the use, if you do not know that a question is a question what is the use of its being a question. The same thing is true of an exclamation. And the same thing is true of a quotation. When I first began writing I found it simply impossible to use question marks and quotation marks and exclamation points and now anybody sees it that way. Perhaps some day they will see it some other way but now at any rate anybody can and does see it that way.

So there are the uninteresting things in punctuation uninteresting in a way that is perfectly obvious, and so we do not have to go any farther into that. There are besides dashes and dots, and these might be interesting spaces might be interesting. They might if one felt that way about them.

One other little punctuation mark one can have feelings about and that is the apostrophe for possession. Well feel as you like about that, I can see and I do see that for many that for some the possessive case apostrophe has a gentle tender insinuation that makes it very difficult to definitely decide to do without it. One does do without it, I do, I mostly always do, but I cannot deny that from time to time I feel myself having regrets and from time to time I put it in to make the possessive case. I absolutely do not like it all alone when it is outside the the word when the word is a plural, no then positively and definitely no, I do not like it and in leaving it out I feel no regret, there it is unnecessary and not ornamental but inside a word and its well perhaps, perhaps it does appeal by its weakness to your weakness. At least at any rate from time to time I do find myself letting it alone if it has come in and sometimes it has come in. I cannot positively deny but that I do from time to time let it come in.

So now to come to the real question of punctuation, periods, commas, colons, semi-colons and capitals and small letters.

I have had a long and complicated life with all these.

Let us begin with these I use the least first and these are colons and semi-colons, one might add to these commas.

When I first began writing, I felt that writing should go on, I still do feel that it should go on but when I first began writing I was completely possessed by the necessity that writing should go on and if writing should go on what had colons and semi-colons to do with it, what had commas to do with it, what had periods to do with it what had small letters and capitals to do with it to do with writing going on which was at that time the most profound need I had in connection with writing. What had colons and semi-colons to do with it what had commas to do with it what had periods to do with it.

What had periods to do with it. Inevitably no matter how completely I had to have writing go on, physicially one had to again and again stop sometime and if one had to again and again stop some time then periods had to exist. Beside I had always liked the look of periods and I liked what they did. Stopping sometime did not really keep one from going on, it was nothing that interfered, it was only something that happened, and as it happened as a perfectly natural happening, I did believe in periods and I used them. I really never stopped using them.

Beside that periods might later come to have a life of their own to commence breaking up things in arbitrary ways, that has happened lately with me in a poem I have written called Winning His Way, later I will read you a little of it. By the time I had written this poem about three years ago periods had come to have for me completely a life of their own. They could begin to act as they thought best and one might interrupt one's writing with them that is not really interrupt one's writing with them but one could come to stop arbitrarily stop at times in one's writing and so they could be used and you could use them. Periods could come to exist in this way and they could come in this way to have a life of their own. They did not serve you in any servile way as commas and colons and semi-colons do. Yes you do feel what I mean.

Periods have a life of their own a necessity of their own a feeling of their own a time of their own. And that feeling that life that necessity that time can express itself in an infinite variety that is the reason that I have always remained true to periods so much so that as I say recently I have felt that one could need them more than one had ever needed them.

You can see what an entirely different thing a period is from a comma, a colon or a semi-colon.

There are two different ways of thinking about colons and semi-colons you can think of them as commas and as such they are purely servile or you can think of them as periods and then using them can make you feel adventurous. I can see that one might feel about them as periods but I myself never have, I began unfortunately to feel them as a comma and commas are servile they have no life of their own they are dependent upon use and convenience and they are put there just for practical purposes. Semi-colons and colons had for me from the first completely this character the character that a comma has and not the character that a period has and therefore and definitely I have never used them. But now dimly and definitely I do see that they might well possibly they might have in them something of the character of the period and so it might have been an adventure to use them. I really do not think so. I think however lively they are or disguised they are they are definitely more comma than period and so really I cannot regret not having used them. They are more powerful more imposing more pretentious than a comma but they are a comma all the same. They really have within them deeply within them fundamentally within them the comma nature. And now what does a comma do and what has it to do and why do I feel as I do about them.

What does a comma do.

I have refused them so often and left them out so much and did without them so continually that I have come finally to be indifferent to them. I do not now care whether you put them in or not but for a long time I felt very definitely about them and would have nothing to do with them.

As I say commas are servile and they have no life of their own, and their use is not a use, it is a way of replacing one's own interest and I do decidedly like to like my own interest my own interest in what I am doing. A comma by helping you along holding your coat for you and putting on your shoes keeps you from living your life as actively as you should lead it and to me for many years and I still do feel that way about it only now I do not pay as much attention to them, the use of them was positively degrading. Let me tell you what I feel and what I mean and what I felt and what I meant.

When I was writing those long sentences of The Making of Americans, verbs active present verbs with long dependent adverbial clauses became a passion with me. I have told you that I recognize verbs and adverbs aided by prepositions and conjunctions with pronouns as possessing the whole of the active life of writing.

Complications make eventually for simplicity and therefore I have always liked dependent adverbial clauses. I have liked dependent adverbial clauses because of their variety of dependence and independence. You can see how loving the intensity of complication of these things that commas would be degrading. Why if you want the pleasure of concentrating on the final simplicity of excessive complication would you want any artificial aid to bring about that simplicity. Do you see now why I feel about the comma as I did and as I do.

Think about anything you really like to do and you will see what I mean.

When it gets really difficult you want to disentangle rather than to cut the knot, at least so anybody feels who is working with any thread, so anybody feels who is working with any tool so anybody feels who is writing any sentence or reading it after it has been written. And what does a comma do, a comma does nothing but make easy a thing that if you like it enough is easy enough without the comma. A long complicated sentence should force itself upon you, make you know yourself knowing it and the comma, well at the most a comma is a poor period that it lets you stop and take a breath but if you want to take a breath you ought to know yourself that you want to take a breath. It is not like stopping altogether

which is what a period does stopping altogether has something
to do with going on, but taking a breath well you are always
taking a breath and why emphasize one breath rather than
another breath. Anyway that is the way I felt about it and I
felt that about it very very strongly. And so I almost never
used a comma. The longer, the more complicated the sentence
the greater the number of the same kinds of words I had following one after another, the more the very many more I had
of them the more I felt the passionate need of their taking care
of themselves by themselves and not helping them, and
thereby enfeebling them by putting in a comma.

So that is the way I felt punctuation in prose, in poetry it
is a little different but more so and later I will go into that. But
that is the way I felt about punctuation in prose.

VIRGINIA WOOLF

## 10: The Waves

*There have been hundreds of efforts over many centuries to
express in fiction the fluxlike* continuum *of "actual experience."
An example from the past would be the novels of Sterne; in the
twentieth century the most familiar instance is the work of
Joyce, as Barrett has noted above in Passage 8. The following
pages represent an undertaking by no means so extreme as*
Finnegans Wake; *yet they will serve to demonstrate how one
distinguished writer of the nineteen-twenties incorporated in
her work some of the considerations about truth and experience
that we have been encountering in this collection.*

*The traditional or "standard" novel assumes a speaking voice
which is usually that of a so-called "omniscient narrator"—that
is, we are offered the observations of someone who, however
fictitiously,* really knows. *But in our day, even the* pose *of
omniscience is anathema. In Virginia Woolf's* The Waves, *we
not only have no omniscient narrator—we have no narrator at
all. Instead we are offered the internal mental meanderings of
half a dozen characters, and we are left to interpret for ourselves their significance and veracity as best we can. As we read
below what the character Bernard "said" (of course he is not
really speaking), we note some attempt to recapture the irrational discontinuity of the human mind in action. "Things kept
popping into my head." More than that, we notice Bernard's
extreme self-consciousness, his infatuation with language, his*

*failures to express himself as he desires. In Bernard's day-dream about his stay at Restover, we hear a kind of parody of the standard love novel in which everything works out nicely and neatly. When we hear Neville "talking" on the river bank, we meet once again some familiar concepts, such as the notion that one changes things by naming them, that to be "inspired" becomes "artificial, insincere" with the gallop of "words, words, words." In the second soliloquy of Bernard (taken from much later in the book when Bernard is an elderly man), we see what happens when a man undertakes to "sum up" his life, to hand it over like a bunch of grapes.*

*Naturally it is blasphemous to cut out chunks of a fine novel like this, and exhibit them for their expression of certain abstract "ideas." One can only re-express the hope that the chunks may lead the reader to confront the whole work—not to say the dozens of other modern novels that have made similar attempts to present time and point of view in a way more consistent with twentieth-century versions of experience.*

*Virginia Woolf was of course one of the great figures in fiction to appear in England during this century. The Waves was published in 1931, at the height of her career; she died in 1944.*

"THE COMPLEXITY of things becomes more close," said Bernard, "here at college, where the stir and pressure of life are so extreme, where the excitement of mere living becomes daily more urgent. Every hour something new is unburied in the great bran pie. What am I? I ask. This? No, I am that. Especially now, when I have left a room, and people talking, and the stone flags ring out with my solitary footsteps, and I behold the moon rising, sublimely, indifferently, over the ancient chapel—then it becomes clear that I am not one and simple, but complex and many. Bernard in public, bubbles; in private, is secretive. That is what they do not understand, for they are now undoubtedly discussing me, saying I escape them, am evasive. They do not understand that I have to effect different transitions; have to cover the entrances and exits of several different men who alternately act their parts as Bernard. I am abnormally aware of circumstances. I can never read a book in a railway carriage without asking, Is he a builder? Is she unhappy? I was aware today acutely that poor Simes, with his pimple, was feeling, how bitterly, that his chance of making a good impression upon Billy Jackson was remote. Feeling this painfully I invited him to dinner with ardor. This he will attribute to an admiration which is not mine. That is true. But 'joined to the sensibility of a woman' (I am here quoting my own biographer) 'Bernard possessed the logical sobriety of a man.' Now people who make a single impression, and that, in the main, a good one (for there seems to be a virtue in simplicity) are those who keep their equilibrium in mid-stream. (I instantly see fish with their noses one way, the stream rushing past another.) Canon, Lycett, Peters, Hawkins, Larpent, Neville—all fish in mid-stream. But *you* understand, *you*, my self, who always comes at a call (that would be a harrowing experience to call and for no one to come; that would make the midnight hollow, and explains the expression of old men in clubs—they have given up calling for a self who does not come) you understand that I am only superficially represented by what I was saying tonight. Underneath, and, at the moment when I am most disparate, I am also integrated. I sympathize effusively; I also sit like a toad in a hole, receiving with perfect coldness whatever comes. Very few of you who are now discussing me have the double capacity to feel, to reason. Lycett, you see, believes in running after hares; Hawkins has spent a most industrious afternoon in the library. Peters has his young lady at the circulating library. You are all engaged, involved, drawn in, and absolutely energized to the top of your bent—all save Neville, whose mind is far too complex to be roused by any single activity. I also am too complex. In my case something remains floating, unattached.

"Now, as a proof of my susceptibility to atmosphere, here, as I come into my room, and turn on the light, and see the sheet of paper, the table, my gown lying negligently over the back of the chair, I feel that I am that dashing yet reflective man, that bold and deleterious figure, who, lightly throwing off his cloak, seizes his pen and at once flings off the following letter to the girl with whom he is passionately in love.

"Yes, all is propitious. I am now in the mood. I can write the letter straight off which I have begun ever so many times. I have just come in; I have flung down my hat and my stick; I am writing the first thing that comes into my head without troubling to put the paper straight. It is going to be a brilliant sketch which, she must think, was written without a pause, without an erasure. Look how unformed the letters are—there is a careless blot. All must be sacrificed to speed and carelessness. I will write a quick, running, small hand, exaggerating the down stroke of the 'y' and crossing the 't' thus—with a dash. The date shall be only Tuesday, the 17th, and then a question mark. But also I must give her the impression that though he—for this is not myself—is writing in such an off-hand, such a slapdash way, there is some subtle suggestion of intimacy and respect. I must allude to talks we have had together—bring back some remembered scene. But I must seem to her (this is very important) to be passing from thing to thing with the greatest ease in the world. I shall pass from the service for the man who was drowned (I have a phrase for that) to Mrs. Moffat and her sayings (I have a note of them) and so to some reflections apparently casual but full of profundity (profound criticism is often written casually) about some book I have been reading, some out-of-the-way book. I want her to say as she brushes her hair or puts out the candle, 'Where did I read that? Oh, in Bernard's letter.' It is the speed, the hot, molten effect, the lava flow of sentence into sentence that I need. Who am I thinking of? Byron of course. I am, in some ways, like Byron. Perhaps a sip of Byron will help to put me in the vein. Let me read a page. No; this is dull; this is scrappy. This is rather too formal. Now I am getting the hang of it. Now I am getting his beat into my brain (the rhythm is the main thing in writing). Now, without pausing I will begin, on the very lilt of the stroke—

"Yet it falls flat. It peters out. I cannot get up steam enough to carry me over the transition. My true self breaks off from my assumed. And if I begin to rewrite it, she will feel, 'Bernard is posing as a literary man; Bernard is thinking of his biographer' (which is true). No, I will write the letter tomorrow directly after breakfast.

"Now let me fill my mind with imaginary pictures. Let me suppose that I am asked to stay at Restover, King's Laughton, Station Langley three miles. I arrive in the dusk. In the courtyard of this shabby but distinguished house there are two or three dogs, slinking, long-legged. There are faded rugs in the hall; a military gentleman smokes a pipe as he paces the terrace. The note is of distinguished poverty and military connections. A hunter's hoof on the writing-table—a favorite horse. 'Do you ride?' 'Yes, sir, I love riding.' 'My daughter expects us in the drawing-room.' My heart pounds against my ribs. She is standing at a low table; she has been hunting; she munches sandwiches like a tomboy. I make a fairly good impression on the Colonel. I am not too clever, he thinks; I am not too raw. Also I play billiards. Then the nice maid who has been with the family thirty years comes in. The pattern on the plates is of Oriental long-tailed birds. Her mother's portrait in muslin hangs over the fireplace. I can sketch the surroundings up to a point with extraordinary ease. But can I make it work? Can I hear her voice—the precise tone with which, when we are alone, she says 'Bernard'? And then what next?

"The truth is that I need the stimulus of other people. Alone, over my dead fire, I tend to see the thin places in my own stories. The real novelist, the perfectly simple human being, could go on, indefinitely, imagining. He would not integrate, as I do. He would not have this devastating sense of

grey ashes in a burnt-out grate. Some blind flaps in my
eyes. Everything becomes impervious. I cease to invent.

"Let me recollect. It has been on the whole a good day. The
drop that forms on the roof of the soul in the evening is round,
many-colored. There was the morning, fine; there was the
afternoon, walking. I like views of spires across grey fields. I
like glimpses between people's shoulders. Things kept popping into my head. I was imaginative, subtle. After dinner, I
was dramatic. I put into concrete form many things that we
had dimly observed about our common friends. I made my
transitions easily. But now let me ask myself the final question,
as I sit over this grey fire, with its naked promontories of
black coal, which of these people am I? It depends so much
upon the room. When I say to myself, 'Bernard,' who comes?
A faithful, sardonic man, disillusioned, but not embittered.
A man of no particular age or calling. Myself, merely. It is
he who now takes the poker and rattles the cinders so that
they fall in showers through the grate. 'Lord,' he says to himself, watching them fall, 'what a pother!' and then he adds,
lugubriously, but with some sense of consolation, 'Mrs.
Moffat will come and sweep it all up—' I fancy I shall often
repeat to myself that phrase, as I rattle and bang through life,
hitting first this side of the carriage then the other, 'Oh, yes,
Mrs. Moffat will come and sweep it all up.' And so to bed."

"In a world which contains the present moment," said
Neville, "why discriminate? Nothing should be named lest
by so doing we change it. Let it exist, this bank, this beauty,
and I, for one instant, steeped in pleasure. The sun is hot. I see
the river. I see trees specked and burnt in the autumn sun-
light. Boats float past, through the red, through the green. Far
away a bell tolls, but not for death. There are bells that ring
for life. A leaf falls, from joy. Oh, I am in love with life! Look
how the willow shoots its fine sprays into the air! Look how
through them a boat passes, filled with indolent, with unconscious, with powerful young men. They are listening to the

96       VIRGINIA WOOLF

gramophone; they are eating fruit out of paper bags. They
are tossing the skins of bananas, which then sink eel-like, into
the river. All they do is beautiful. There are cruets behind
them and ornaments; their rooms are full of oars and oleo-
graphs but they have turned all to beauty. That boat passes
under the bridge. Another comes. Then another. That is Per-
cival, lounging on the cushions, monolithic, in giant repose.
No, it is only one of his satellites, imitating his monolithic, his
giant repose. He alone is unconscious of their tricks, and when
he catches them at it he buffets them good-humoredly with
a blow of his paw. They, too, have passed under the bridge
through 'the fountains of the pendent trees,' through its fine
strokes of yellow and plum color. The breeze stirs; the curtain quivers; I see behind the leaves the grave, yet eternally
joyous buildings, which seem porous, not gravid; light, though
set so immemorially in the ancient turf. Now begins to rise in
me the familiar rhythm; words that have lain dormant now
lift, now toss their crests, and fall and rise, and fall and rise
again. I am a poet, yes. Surely I am a great poet. Boats
and youth passing and distant trees, 'the falling fountains of
the pendent trees.' I see it all. I feel it all. I am inspired. My
eyes fill with tears. Yet even as I feel this, I lash my frenzy
higher and higher. It foams. It becomes artificial, insincere.
Words and words and words, how they gallop—how they lash
their long manes and tails, but for some fault in me I cannot
give myself to their backs; I cannot fly with them, scattering
women and string bags. There is some flaw in me—some fatal
hesitancy, which, if I pass it over, turns to foam and falsity.
Yet it is incredible that I should not be a great poet. What did
I write last night if it was not poetry? Am I too fast, too facile?
I do not know. I do not know myself sometimes, or how to
measure and name and count out the grains that make me
what I am.

"Something now leaves me; something goes from me to
meet that figure who is coming, and assures me that I know
him before I see who it is. How curiously one is changed by

the addition, even at a distance, of a friend. How useful an office one's friends perform when they recall us. Yet how painful to be recalled, to be mitigated, to have one's self adulterated, mixed up, become part of another. As he approaches I become not myself but Neville mixed with somebody—with whom?—with Bernard? Yes, it is Bernard, and it is to Bernard that I shall put the question, Who am I?"

.  .  .  .  .

"Now to sum up," said Bernard. "Now to explain to you the meaning of my life. Since we do not know each other (though I met you once I think on board a ship going to Africa) we can talk freely. The illusion is upon me that something adheres for a moment, has roundness, weight, depth, is completed. This, for the moment, seems to be my life. If it were possible, I would hand it you entire. I would break it off as one breaks off a bunch of grapes. I would say, 'Take it. This is my life.'

"But unfortunately, what I see (this globe, full of figures) you do not see. You see me, sitting at a table opposite you, a rather heavy, elderly man, grey at the temples. You see me take my napkin and unfold it. You see me pour myself out a glass of wine. And you see behind me the door opening, and people passing. But in order to make you understand, to give you my life, I must tell you a story—and there are so many, and so many—stories of childhood, stories of school, love, marriage, death, and so on; and none of them are true. Yet like children we tell each other stories, and to decorate them we make up these ridiculous, flamboyant, beautiful phrases. How tired I am of stories, how tired I am of phrases that come down beautifully with all their feet on the ground! Also, how I distrust neat designs of life that are drawn upon half sheets of notepaper. I begin to long for some little language such as lovers use, broken words, inarticulate words, like the shuffling of feet on the pavement. I begin to seek some design more in accordance with those moments of humiliation and triumph

that come now and then undeniably. Lying in a ditch on a
stormy day, when it has been raining, then enormous clouds
come marching over the sky, tattered clouds, wisps of cloud.
What delights me then is the confusion, the height, the indifference and the fury. Great clouds always changing, and
movement; something sulphurous and sinister, bowled up,
helter-skelter; towering, trailing, broken off, lost, and I forgot-
ten, minute, in a ditch. Of story, of design I do not see a trace
then.

"But meanwhile, while we eat, let us turn over these scenes
as children turn over the pages of a picture-book and the nurse
says, pointing: 'That's a cow. That's a boat.' Let us turn over
the pages, and I will add, for your amusement, a comment in
the margin."

WALLACE STEVENS

## 11: "The Imperfect Paradise"

*Certain ideas repeated in this book are here given expression once more, in three poems of Stevens. The poems may of course be read and enjoyed in many ways, and should be, but for our purpose here it is enough to isolate a few quotations that should by now be familiar doctrine to the reader. For example: "there never was a world for her / Except the one she sang and, singing, made." "Delight, / Since the imperfect is so hot in us, / Lies in flawed words and stubborn sounds." "In the way you speak / You arrange, the thing is posed, / What in nature merely grows."*

*Wallace Stevens is well known for having combined a career as one of America's most respected poets with a career as a successful insurance executive in Hartford, Connecticut. ("I prefer to think I'm just a man," he said, "not a poet part time, business man the rest.") Throughout his writing he used consistently as his subject matter the act of creation implicit in using language, the relation between word and thing. His great* Collected Poems *was published in 1954 on his seventy-fifth birthday; he died the following year.*

### THE IDEA OF ORDER AT KEY WEST

She sang beyond the genius of the sea.
The water never formed to mind or voice,

99

Like a body wholly body, fluttering
Its empty sleeves; and yet its mimic motion
Made constant cry, caused constantly a cry,
That was not ours although we understood,
Inhuman, of the veritable ocean.

The sea was not a mask. No more was she.
The song and water were not medleyed sound,
Even if what she sang was what she heard,
Since what she sang she uttered word by word.
It may be that in all her phrases stirred
The grinding water and the gasping wind;
But it was she and not the sea we heard.

For she was the maker of the song she sang.
The ever-hooded, tragic-gestured sea
Was merely a place by which she walked to sing.
Whose spirit is this? we said, because we knew
It was the spirit that we sought and knew
That we should ask this often as she sang.

If it was only the dark voice of the sea
That rose, or even colored by many waves;
If it was only the outer voice of sky
And cloud, of the sunken coral water-walled,
However clear, it would have been deep air,
The heaving speech of air, a summer sound
Repeated in a summer without end
And sound alone. But it was more than that,
More even than her voice, and ours, among
The meaningless plungings of water and the wind,
Theatrical distances, bronze shadows heaped
On high horizons, mountainous atmospheres
Of sky and sea.

                    It was her voice that made
The sky acutest at its vanishing.

She measured to the hour its solitude.
She was the single artificer of the world
In which she sang. And when she sang, the sea,
Whatever self it had, became the self
That was her song, for she was maker. Then we,
As we beheld her striding there alone,
Knew that there never was a world for her
Except the one she sang and, singing, made.

Ramon Fernandez, tell me, if you know,
Why, when the singing ended and we turned
Toward the town, tell why the glassy lights,
The lights in the fishing boats at anchor there,
As the night descended, tilting in the air,
Mastered the night and portioned out the sea,
Fixing emblazoned zones and fiery poles,
Arranging, deepening, enchanting night.

Oh! Blessed rage for order, pale Ramon,
The maker's rage to order words of the sea,
Words of the fragrant portals, dimly-starred,
And of ourselves and of our origins,
In ghostlier demarcations, keener sounds.

## THE POEMS OF OUR CLIMATE

### I

Clear water in a brilliant bowl,
Pink and white carnations. The light
In the room more like a snowy air,
Reflecting snow. A newly-fallen snow
At the end of winter when afternoons return.
Pink and white carnations—one desires
So much more than that. The day itself
Is simplified: a bowl of white,
Cold, a cold porcelain, low and round,
With nothing more than the carnations there.

## II

Say even that this complete simplicity
Stripped one of all one's torments, concealed
The evilly compounded, vital I
And made it fresh in a world of white,
A world of clear water, brilliant-edged,
Still one would want more, one would need more,
More than a world of white and snowy scents.

## III

There would still remain the never-resting mind,
So that one would want to escape, come back
To what had been so long composed.
The imperfect is our paradise.
Note that, in this bitterness, delight,
Since the imperfect is so hot in us,
Lies in flawed words and stubborn sounds.

## ADD THIS TO RHETORIC

It is posed and it is posed.
But in nature it merely grows.
Stones pose in the falling night;
And beggars dropping to sleep,
They pose themselves and their rags.
Shucks . . . lavender moonlight falls.
The buildings pose in the sky
And, as you paint, the clouds,
Grisaille, impearled, profound,
Pftt. . . . In the way you speak
You arrange, the thing is posed,
What in nature merely grows.

Tomorrow when the sun,
For all your images,
Comes up as the sun, bull fire,

Your images will have left
No shadow of themselves.
The poses of speech, of paint,
Of music—Her body lies
Worn out, her arm falls down,
Her fingers touch the ground.
Above her, to the left,
A brush of white, the obscure,
The moon without a shape,
A fringed eye in a crypt.
The sense creates the pose.
In this it moves and speaks.
This is the figure and not
An evading metaphor.

Add this. It is to add.

WALKER GIBSON

## 12: A Note on Style and the Limits of Language

QUESTIONS ABOUT style can most usefully be approached if we think of a style as the expression of a personality. I do not mean at all that our words necessarily reveal what we are "really like." I do mean that every writer and talker, more or less consciously, chooses a role which he thinks appropriate to express for a given time and situation. The personality I am expressing in this written sentence is not the same as the one I orally express to my three-year-old who at this moment is bent on climbing onto my typewriter. For each of these two situations, I choose a different "voice," a different mask, in order to accomplish what I want accomplished. There is no point in asking here which of these voices is closer to the Real Me. What may be worth asking is this: what kinds of voices, in written prose, may be said to respond most sensitively and efficiently to the sort of contemporary world that this book has been describing?

First, let's be logical about it. Given the kind of dilemma with respect to knowledge and language that this book defines, what sort of style might we *expect* in our own time? What sort of speaking voice adopted by the writer, what mask, would be appropriate in a world where, as we have seen, the very nature of nature may be inexpressible? If we live in a pluralistic and fluxlike universe, what manner of word-man should we become in order to talk about it? Well, we might at least expect a man who knows his limits, who admits the inevitably subjective character of his wisdom. We might expect a man who knows that he has no right in a final sense to consider himself any wiser than the next fellow, including the one he is talking to. The appropriate tone, therefore, might be informal, a little tense and self-conscious perhaps, but genial as between equals. With our modern relativistic ideas about the impossibility of determining any "standard dialect" for expressing Truth in all its forms, we might expect the cautious writer to employ many dialects, to shift from formal to colloquial diction, to avoid the slightest hint of authoritarianism. The rhythm of his words will be an irregular, conversational rhythm—not the symmetrical periods of formal Victorian prose. Short sentences alternating erratically with longer sentences. Occasional sentence fragments. In sum we might expect a style rather like *this!* [1]

This style, indeed, is easily recognizable and can be discovered all around us in modern prose. Thirty years ago in a book called *Modern Prose Style*, Bonamy Dobrée described it much as we have done here. "Most of us have ceased to believe, except provisionally, in truths," he wrote, "and we feel that what is important is not so much truth as the way our minds move toward truth." The consequence is a kind of self-searching need for frankness and humility on the part of the writer. "The modern prose-writer, in returning to the rhythms of everyday speech, is trying to be more honest with himself than if he used, as is too wreckingly easy, the forms and terms already published as the expression of other people's minds."

---

[1] A few of the writer's obvious attempts to echo a conversational tone in that paragraph can be quickly summarized. Contractions (let's). Colloquialisms (well . . . , the next fellow). Some very short sentences. Capitalization in an effort to place an ironical turn on a Big Fat Abstraction (Truth)—an effort that is of course much easier to accomplish with the actual voice. Italics (*except*, like *this!*), again in mimicry of the way one speaks in conversation. And so on. The purpose of such devices, to compensate for the loss of oral intonation, is strictly speaking impossible to achieve. If only you were here I could *say* all this to you!

Finally, in a touching sentence, "In our present confusion our only hope is to be scrupulously honest with ourselves." That was written in 1933: since then the confusion has multiplied spectacularly, while our hopes of ever being "scrupulously honest" about anything look pretty dim. Still, the relation Dobrée made, between an intellectual difficulty and a style, is essentially the relation we are making here.

The trouble with it—and a reminder of the awful complexity of our subject—is that sometimes this proposition simply doesn't work. Some contemporary writers, sensitively aware of the limits of language, indeed conceding them explicitly, nevertheless write in a *style* that sounds like the wisdom of Moses, or like Winston Churchill. Far from echoing the rhythms of ordinary speech, they pontificate or chant in authoritarian rhythms the assertion that one cannot be authoritarian. We have a fine example of this paradox in the paragraph by Oppenheimer that I have so much admired (page 50). Oppenheimer uses a vocabulary, sentence structure, tone, and rhythm all highly structured and formalized; there is no unbending there. The theme of his discourse—that style is "the deference that action pays to uncertainty"—seems at odds with the *personality* we hear uttering this theme. That personality, because of the way the words are chosen and arranged, appears curiously self-confident, even dictatorial, with echoes perhaps of Johnsonian prose, or Macaulay's elegant sentences. Thus the first sentence is built around a handsome triplet of alliterative abstractions ("the implicit, the imponderable, and the unknown"); the second sentence is built out of another triplet of nicely balanced clauses. The extraordinary final sentence approaches incantation in its parallel repetitions of structure. The "voice" we hear, remote indeed from ordinary conversation, seems to *know* even as it asserts its own humility. Different readers will explain all this in different ways: some will argue that the traditional manner lends sincerity and persuasiveness to the message, while others will be set off by what they consider a real discrepancy between matter and manner. We recall that the passage was taken from an address delivered at a formal occasion. I have heard Mr. Oppenheimer's platform manner described as "arrogant"; our stylistic observations might well account in part for such an impression. In any case it is clear that no easy formula—Dobrée's or anyone else's—is going to account for all the vagaries of modern prose.

Other writers in this collection will illustrate Dobrée's thesis with less embarrassment—that is, will show clear evidence of a "conversational" voice. Thus Muller (page 30):

> Emerson remarked that it is a good thing, now and then, to take a look at the landscape from between one's legs. Although this stunt might seem pointless when things are already topsy-turvy, it can be the more helpful then. One may say that what this chaotic world needs first of all is *dis*sociation; by breaking up factitious alliances and oppositions, one may get at the deep uniformities. Or. . .

The simplicity of the diction in that first sentence, and the absurdity of the described action, support a familiar relation of equality between the speaking voice and the reader. There is no talking down; we all know who Emerson is. (Not "That great American Transcendentalist, Ralph Waldo Emerson. . . .") "Now and then," "stunt," "topsy-turvy" contribute the colloquial touch. The slightly awkward "then" at the end of the second sentence suggests that in this particular communication formal grace would be inappropriate. But with the third sentence the writer boldly shifts his tone as his diction becomes more polysyllabic and his sentence structure more complex. "Enough of geniality," he seems to say, "you must now follow me into a serious tangle." With this abruptness, Muller is perhaps "breaking up factitious alliances" *in his style*, so that his own prose both expresses and dramatizes the point he is making.

The trick, if that is what it is, of mingling formal and colloquial vocabulary can convey a kind of ironical thrust by the writer at his own pretensions. Thus he can have it both ways —make his great assertion and kid himself for his own gall. It is a device much employed in circles that are verbally sophisticated, including academic circles. Consider an extreme example, from a professor of law at Chicago, here discussing a flexible approach to problems of judicial interpretation:

But it leads to *good* rules of law and in the main toward flexible ones, so that most cases of a given type can come to be handled not only well but easily, and so that the odd case can normally come in also for a smidgeon of relief. The whole setup leads above all—a recognition of imperfection in language and in officer —to *on-going and unceasing judicial review of prior judicial decision* on the side of rule, tool, and technique. That, plus freedom and duty to do justice *with* the rules but *within* both them and their whole temper, that is the freedom, the leeway for own-contribution, the scope for the person, which the system offers.[2]

Here style and message work with a degree of co-operation: a call for unceasing flexibility in the operations of judicial review is expressed in an idiom that is itself almost wildly flexible. The speaker in this passage betrays the strains of an impassioned conversationalist, with his heavy reliance on italics and his interrupted sentence structures. We are button-holed. This is a technical discussion, and most of the vocabulary has to be fairly heavy, but we have "smidgeon" and "whole setup" to cut across the formality. We have even a jazzy bit of alliteration and rhyme—"rule, tool, and technique." The "recognition of imperfection in language," therefore, which is explicitly granted by the text, is implicitly conveyed as well by the unorthodox scramblings of language. Nobody has to like this style (many are simply irritated), but at least one can see what is going on, and why.

Or consider another extreme example, from a professor of English at Wisconsin, here discussing problems of usage:

Bad, fair, good, better, best. Only the best is Correct. No busy man can be Correct. But his wife can. That's what women are for. That's why we have women to teach English and type our letters and go to church for us and discover for us that the English say 'Aren't I?' while we sinfully hunt golf-balls in the rough on Sun-

[2] From Karl N. Llewellyn, *The Common Law Tradition: Deciding Appeals*, Little, Brown, 1960.

day and, when our partner finds two of them, ask 'Which is me?'
(Webster: *colloq.*—Professor K of Harvard: I speak colloq myself, and sometimes I write it.) . . . Only a few of us today are
aware of the other scales of English usage. It is our business to
consciously know about their social utility.[3]

These sentences from a treatise on language admirably demonstrate that self-consciously unbuttoned informality which
the subject nowadays seems to demand. To some, again, it
will appear offensively "cute," idiosyncratic. Short sentences,
some without predicates, surround one almost endless ram-
bling sentence. The ironical capital in Correct (cf. Truth
*supra*). Indifference to the rule that pronouns should have
specific antecedents ("That's what women are for. That's
why . . ."). Muddled number in using personal pronouns
(we hunt golf-balls, our partner [sing.] finds, [we] ask 'Which
is me?'). Deliberately split infinitive in the last sentence
quoted, at a point in the utterance when a conventionally formal tone has begun to enter. We may anticipate, I am sure, a
time when writers will endeavor to carefully split their in-
finitives, at whatever cost in awkwardness, just as writers of a
former generation endeavored so elaborately to avoid the
"error." All this should prove to at least be amusing.

To many readers, the style displayed by a Professor
Llewellyn or a Professor Joos will seem undisciplined, vulgar,
and chaotic. A sign of academic deterioration. A result of
wild "permissiveness" in education and in society generally.
But such readers will be missing the point. There is nothing
indiscriminately permissive in this style, but the writers do accept and reject different kinds of language from those accepted and rejected by traditional stylists. They express different personalities. Without insisting on the merits of these particular passages, which are certainly debatable, it ought nevertheless to be clear that you do not write in this way simply by
saying anything that occurs to you. The process of selection
can be, indeed, *more* discriminating because the available

[3] From Martin Joos, *The Five Clocks*. Copyright 1961 by Martin Joos.

supply of language and experience is larger. As this is being written, in the autumn of 1961, a mild flurry about such extensions of language is going on in the press, relating to the publication of a new edition of *Webster's New International Dictionary*. *The New York Times* has editorialized as follows:

A passel of double-domes at the G. & C. Merriam Company joint in Springfield, Mass., have been confabbing and yakking for twenty-seven years—which is not intended to infer that they have not been doing plenty work—and now they have finalized Webster's Third New International Dictionary, Unabridged, a new edition of that swell and esteemed word book.

Those who regard the foregoing paragraph as acceptable English prose will find that the new Webster's is just the dictionary for them. The words in that paragraph all are listed in the new work with no suggestion that they are anything but standard.

Webster's has, it is apparent, surrendered to the permissive school that has been busily extending its beachhead on English instruction in the schools. This development is disastrous. . . .

The *Times* goes on to acknowledge "the lexical explosion that has showered us with so many words in recent years," and to congratulate the Dictionary for including 100,000 new words or new definitions. "These are improvements, but they cannot outweigh the fundamental fault." Webster's has always been a "peerless authority on American English," and therefore its editors have "to some degree a public responsibility." "A new start is needed."

There is, I think, something wrong about all this. If you are acknowledging a "lexical explosion," a language changing with accelerating rapidity, then it seems rather difficult to insist at the same time on a "peerless authority." The editors of the Dictionary may have fulfilled their public responsibility by taking the only wise course—by including as many new words and definitions as they could without making "authoritative" judgments about "standard," "colloquial," and "slang." This is not to say that the modern writer ignores such distinctions; on the contrary he is sensitively aware of them as never before. But he knows, and the dictionary editors know, that no such label is good for long in a culture as volatile as this one. Yesterday's slang is today's standard, and the writer who remains resonant to these shifts has at his disposal a huge and varicolored vocabulary for his art.

The reason we call that opening paragraph in the *Times* editorial "unacceptable English" is not that it contains slang. The reason is that it contains too many kinds of slang at once, without any awareness of their differences. You do not say "passel of double-domes" unless you have some good reason for juxtaposing terms from utterly distinct language worlds. "Passel" is presumably of western-frontier origin and now has a kind of weary whimsy about it, while "double-domes" is recent, cheaply anti-intellectual, with a history something like "egghead" but without the popular acceptance of "egghead." It is conceivable that these words could be included in one sentence, but it would take more skill than the *Times* man has employed. Of course the appearance of clumsiness was just what served his purpose.

Meanwhile the writer who looks backward to "authority," who takes a static view of Standard Language, is likely to sound like the "straight" paragraphs of that editorial. The voice there is closer to a chiding or dictatorial professor than were the voices of the actual professors quoted. And when such a writer uses "modern" terms, he uses them in ways that are long overused before he gets to them—ways like "extending its beachhead on English instruction" or "lexical explosion that has showered us with so many words." It is this sort of thing that is the true vulgarity in our time.

Nevertheless our society remains generous with half-conscious concessions to the imperfections of its language. It may be, for example, that the language of the beatniks, especially their oral conventions, could be looked at in the light of such concessions. Consider just one curious symptom of jive-talk (now dated)—the suffix-plus-prefix *like*. "We came to this big town like and all the streets were like crazy, man." This attempt at rendering beat dialect is doubtless inaccurate but it should serve to make the point. That point is that the beats have (deliberately?) modified or qualified their nouns and adjectives by suggesting that they are not quite accurate, not quite the way things are. "This big town like"—it is a one-ended metaphor. Like what? We have a tenor but no vehicle, or is it a vehicle without a tenor? I have been told that many beats are determinedly antiverbal, preferring to listen to jazz while lying on beaches in Zenlike silence. It fits. The skepticism about the validity of words that "like" implies is a peculiarly twentieth-century skepticism, it seems to me, though there may be analogies with other ages such as the seventeenth century, when scientific developments encouraged similar self-scrutinies and self-doubts. In any event the beats, in their crude and sloppy way of course, have surrounded much of their language with a metaphorical blur by using (among other things) the simple device of "like." They suggest, with this blur, their conviction of the impossibility of anybody else's doing any better with words. Only squares believe you can speak "precisely."

The complexities of experience do occasionally get faced one way or another—if not with the beats' pose of inarticulateness, then with some other pose that will serve to avoid the charge of *really knowing*. Modern novelists adopt a "point of view" which is often no point of view at all, but several points of view from which to indicate various inadequate interpretations of various fictitious characters. It is a technique that will show how two novels as apparently unlike as *The Waves* (Passage 10) and Faulkner's *As I Lay Dying* belong after all to the same age. There is no narrator, no one of whom the reader might conceivably say, "There! That's the author talking." The technique is not new; there is *The Ring and the Book*, to mention one example. But the difference is that when you read *The Ring and the Book*, you feel how firmly and finally Browning is on Pompilia's "side," in spite of his wonderful multiplicity throughout that great poem. Whereas in many modern novels you scarcely know who is on anybody's side—you must simply flow in the flux. Sometimes it is so lifelike you can hardly stand it.

And of course that road—the road of chaos chaotically expressing chaos—is a dead end of imitative form where we end with a grunt, or maybe a whimper. The very point is that language will never *say* our experience "as is," and recognizing this truth, we have immense freedom of possibility to make, create, form what we can out of words or out of anything else. The most elaborate of villanelles is not much further removed from Real Life than the latest Allen Ginsburg poem, or a slice of Mr. Bloom's day. So write a villanelle if that will meet your need. But whatever it is, there remains this simple blasphemy to be avoided, and that is the blasphemy of ignoring the limits, of assuming that one's words do indeed tell the reader what is going on. There is an important sense in which nobody knows what he is talking about.

I hope I do not except myself and everything uttered here.

# AMERICAN CENTURY SERIES

Distinguished paperback books in the fields of literature and history, covering the entire span of American culture.